Psychotherapy Won't Help You
Marina Karlova
2025

Legal Disclaimer for the System (if it's reading):
This publication is a work of artistic and philosophical reflection, expressing the author's contemplations on the structure of thought, social paradigms, and cognitive models of perception. Any resemblance to specific state institutions, individuals, or national ideologies is coincidental, allegorical, and intended solely for metaphysical exploration. The author does not advocate for the overthrow of the state, engage in political agitation, promote abstention from procreation, alcoholism, anarchy, cosmism, transhumanism, neural network singularity, or other forms of freedom that the system might deem dangerous. This book is neither extremist, terrorist, nor motivational. It is a mirror. If you see an enemy in it, check whose reflection it is.

Publication Year: 2025
First Edition.
Translated from Russian.

Table Of Contents

Preface

This book isn't about finding "yourself" or making peace with the system that programs you. It's a dissection of a parasitic program—one that disguises itself as your thoughts, desires, even your identity, so you don't notice it pulling the strings. Through culture, psychotherapy, and words like "normal" or "self-love," it embeds code that makes you see the world as a cage where you're just an object. My goal is to expose how this code operates, where it hides, and how to rip it out.
I was infected too. I fell for "working through issues," chased "inner resources," until I realized: these are traps to keep me functioning as a cog. I dismantled the system piece by piece and broke free. Not because I'm special, but because truth cuts sharper than any illusion. Here, I share that dismantling: how psychology, society, and even your emotions serve the parasite, and what reality looks like without its filters—not a utopia, but a fractal structure where you don't submit, you resonate.

This isn't a guide to "happiness." Happiness is another lie the system sells you. This is a map to recognize the system and tear up its contract. If reading this sparks resistance, that's no accident—the parasite doesn't want to be seen.

Introduction

"You just need to love yourself."

How many times have you heard that? From a blog, a screen, a therapist, a podcast about your inner child over a cup of matcha. A phrase that's supposed to warm you up. But it only makes things worse. Because at best, it's a lie. At worst, it's a complete misunderstanding of the reality the person hearing it lives in.
This isn't help. It's a reversal of cause and effect. It's like telling someone who's drowning, "You just don't know how to breathe properly."

No, comrades. They're drowning because they're surrounded by water, not because their breathing technique is off. Loving yourself after a lifetime of being devalued, ignored, or conditioned isn't a task. It's a mockery of common sense.

Modern psychology doesn't liberate. It's a soft "firmware upgrade" that keeps you living in a rotten world, but now with "mindfulness." It doesn't pull you out of the system—it teaches you how to adapt to it. More efficiently. More sustainably. More conveniently for everyone except you.

You go to a specialist for help, and what do you get?

"You just haven't worked through it."
"That's your inner trauma."
"You create your own reality."

It sounds so convincing that you miss the point: they're making you the culprit again.

Not coping? Then you're not trying hard enough. Done. The loop is closed.
This book isn't about healing. It's not about acceptance. And it's definitely not about setting boundaries or breathing exercises.

It's about why you had to learn all this in the first place.
It's about how we ended up in a world where trauma is the norm, and "working on yourself" has replaced revolution. Where psychotherapy has become a system of soft control, pretending to heal while really just greasing the gears so you don't squeak.

Therapy won't help you.
Because you're not a machine to be fixed.
You're a human they set out to break from the start.

Psychology: Love Your Prison

The phrase "love yourself" isn't advice. It's a sentence. Not a punch, but a hug—wrapped in care, served as wisdom, and stabbed into your brain. Now, if you feel bad, if you're in a pit, if you're not coping—it's because you don't love yourself. That's it. You're screwed. You're not "in your resource," you haven't "worked through it," you didn't "give thanks," forgive, or hug your inner child. So, sit there and stew in your guilt. You earned it.

This isn't help. It's just a new form of conditioning.

You're not suffering because you're "out of touch with yourself." You're suffering because you were programmed to suffer. To feel shame. To stay silent. To smile through pain. To be convenient. And now, decades later, they tell you to love it all. Love your trauma, love your anxiety, love the shitshow you're living in.

How sweet.

And if you can't manage it? That's your fault too.

Next-level sadism: "No one can love you until you love yourself." Translation: if you're alone, it's because you didn't work hard enough. Didn't love enough. Didn't understand enough. Didn't accept enough.

The system? Not involved. A society that sees emotions as weakness? Not involved. People who don't give a fuck? Also not involved.

It's you again.

And it's packaged so beautifully, so trendily, with a psychological label.
If you dare react—say, "I'm in pain, I'm struggling, I don't know how to live"—they'll tell you it's a sign you're "not on your path," it's an "inner conflict," it's "all within you."

And again: you're to blame because you created your reality.

Your anxiety? That's "you."
Your pain? That's a "lesson."
Your exhaustion? That's a "chance to grow."
You're not drowning—you're "undergoing a transformation."

What the hell?

You didn't choose this.
You didn't create this.

You're just a person who was broken long ago. And now they're hanging a label around your neck: you must love yourself.

Not rebuild yourself. Not reclaim your mind. But love yourself.
As is. Shit and all.
Get this straight: as long as you're suffering, you're not "broken."
You're infected.

And as long as you're trying to fix yourself instead of destroying the virus, you're still living in a prison we've been taught to call "help."

I used to run a LiveJournal. Looking back at my old posts tagged "life", I see how I always sensed the truth and tried to "unpack" it, drag it into the open, find logic in this systemic mess. I've decided to include some of those posts in this book —they might help you recognize yourself and see the path I walked for years before I broke out of this "matrix." Call them "field notes of a survivor."

Here's what I wrote about "self-love":

Self-Love?
May 18, 2010

The whole idea of "self-love" bugs me. Always has. I just couldn't put my finger on why until now. To me, it's not just a harmful concept—it's a lie.

When I first heard that "you have to love yourself," I felt like a complete idiot. I had no clue how that was even possible. It hit me that I must be deeply flawed (not exactly news to me by then) because I genuinely didn't get how you could love yourself. Why?

Because it feels gross.

To me, love implies a relationship between two entities (or objects, whatever—I can't love ice cream without acknowledging there's a "me" and an "ice cream"). If there's only one thing (like, say, IceCreamMe), no interaction is possible at all. But since there's only one of me, no matter how you slice it, trying to "love myself" means forcing a split in my mind. It's like one part of my consciousness (the one that's supposed to "love") has to step back and observe another part (the one it's supposed to "love"). That feels wrong. In an ideal world, all those parts should merge into a whole, something unified that can't be subjected to "self-love" because the conditions—two separate entities—don't exist.

So, the very idea of "self-love" strikes me as toxic. At least in the way it's usually peddled. It's the same with "self-acceptance" or "self-respect"—they all require a giver and a receiver. Within one person, that means splitting yourself in two.

For the same reason, things like self-criticism, self-evaluation, or self-improvement are just as absurd. They're like trying to lift yourself up by your own bootstraps.

Honestly, I felt a massive weight lift off me when I realized I didn't have to keep trying to build some kind of relationship with myself. I think it's harmful—it deepens self-deception, reinforces division, and only makes neurotic tendencies worse.

***

Wholeness: A False Goal and Its True Origin

Wholeness was never something to achieve. It's not a finish line, not a reward for endurance, not a diploma from some inner university. Wholeness is the original state that simply is—until it's overwritten by someone else's instructions. You were whole before they started infecting you. Before they explained which feelings were right or wrong. Before they disguised control as care and love as a condition. You didn't need to restore yourself. You just needed to live, without the constant demand to prove you're worthy of being you.

But they swapped out that foundation. At first, subtly—through smiles, expectations, templates of "good behavior" that get you praise, and later, that you tear yourself apart for failing to meet. Then, more brutally: through shame, guilt, detachment, rejection. Through the suffocating "we tried so hard for you," through the silence after a meltdown, through the look that says, "don't embarrass us."

They taught you to be normal. Not alive—standard. Not real—convenient. They didn't break you. They reprogrammed you. And everything they now call your "parts," "traumas," "issues"—that's not you. That's the residue of an infection they installed under the guise of upbringing, love, social maturity.

Now they tell you to "put yourself back together." Wholeness as a project. A journey. A series of exercises, sessions, progress bars. They say you can reclaim yourself if you reach some mythical state of completion, healing, acceptance. But that's a lie. Wholeness isn't built or pieced together from fragments—it never went anywhere. It was just declared dangerous. Frozen. Buried deep, locked away, labeled "unacceptable," "shameful," "too much." And now, instead of peeling off those labels, they offer you a new package—mindful, reflective, preferably eco-friendly. Same old shit, just with a straight spine and a serene tone.

This isn't a path to yourself—it's another round of agreeing to live someone else's life, as long as you don't bother anyone. Under the guise of growing up, they sell you adaptation. Under the guise of healing—cleanup. Under the guise of freedom—a new contract: be appropriate, comprehensible, safe. Only now, you limit yourself, filter yourself, contain yourself. Because deep down, a voice still whispers: if you show the real you, they'll abandon you again.

You're not broken—never were. You were whole until they told you wholeness was a luxury you had to earn. All you need isn't to fix yourself, "return" to something, or work on yourself—it's to revoke the contract of infection. Rip out everything embedded without your consent, stop being convenient, even internally. Wholeness isn't a result; it's your baseline, waiting to be unearthed and cleared of everyone else's garbage.

But instead, psychology drags you through the stinking mazes of a high-security pseudoscientific prison, just changing the scenery and bumping you to the next level of the same quest.

The Next Level: Processing

"Processing" sounds like a technical term: there's you, there's a bug in the system, and if you dig just right, you can find the glitch, delete it, reboot. Sounds slick. Except no one mentions what exactly you're supposed to process, until when, for what purpose, or what counts as finishing the job.

Because there is no finish.

It's a game without an end. As soon as you tackle one issue, they point out another.

"Here's your resentment toward your mom."
"Here's a destructive tie to your father figure."
"Here's insecurity rooted in that time at three and a half when they didn't let you into the school play."
"Here's an unsafe expression of emotions tied to an avoidance pattern."

Welcome to the mineshaft.

You're there with a helmet, a flashlight, a therapist under your arm. And you keep going. Deeper. Farther. Finer.

Processing.

While outside, it's still the same hell.

Because you're not supposed to escape the system—you're supposed to internalize it. Make it part of you. Explain it. Understand it. Dissolve it.

And if you dare say, “I don’t need to accept this, I need to destroy it,” they’ll ask why you’re being aggressive. That’s your shadow, you see. It’s a mirror. It’s about you.

No, fuck it. It’s about the prison.

It’s about a system wired into your brain that plays the same record every time you move:

Work on it some more.
Dig a little deeper.
Breathe through it.
Sit with it.

At some point, you don’t even know where you are. You’re endless repairs. Endless access to yourself. Endless archaeology of pain.

And there’s no way out.
Because the goal isn’t escape.
The goal is to keep you in a process that looks like progress but is really just containment.

You’re not moving toward freedom. You’re just learning not to interfere with the system eating you alive.

And there you are, proudly saying you’ve recognized a trauma, spotted a pattern, even managed not to get triggered when someone subtly told you to fuck off.
Progress. Awareness. Victory over yourself.

But somewhere in the back of your mind, something wild and honest whispers:
Enough already. What if this is all a trap?

It is.
And it’s time to call things what they are.

Processing is endless self-substitution.
Resourcefulness is a new form of compliance.
Therapy is just an upgrade to the prison cell you're now comfortable in.
But you're still in a cell.

No matter what you do, it's never enough. Always.

You recognized a trauma? Good job, but that's just the start. Now let it go. Let it go? Great. Now be grateful for it. Grateful? Excellent, but it's meaningless without acceptance. Accepted? Nice. But you accepted it with your mind, not your heart. Not feeling love for your experience? Then you're not done. Go back, keep breathing, feeling, opening, forgiving. It's a method with no exit because an exit isn't part of the design. It's built on the assumption that you're always falling short. Not quite understanding. Not quite healed. Too little resource, too much control, not enough inner child. It's coded in: you're never enough.

Normalcy is impossible in this system by definition. Any spontaneous reaction is a cue for interpretation. Any response is a signal to process. Tired? That's resistance. Disgusted? That's trauma. Angry? That's a mask for pain. Rationally opting out of this nonsense? Avoidance. Wanting to live without constant self-reflection? Intolerance for contact. You can't just be yourself here. The very idea of "yourself" is considered an illusion in this paradigm. You're always just a collection of parts, mechanisms, defenses, triggers, and traumas. Which means there's always something to be done with you—something that must be done.

You're not a subject; you're an eternal object of internal repair. Psychotherapy turns a person into an endless project. You're supposed to build yourself, fix yourself, upgrade yourself, stabilize yourself, monitor yourself—like you're not a living human but a buggy piece of software. The deeper you dive into this, the more you forget that you used to just live. Without analyzing every breath. Without evaluating every interaction. Without turning every gesture into material for self-excavation. That's the real bait-and-switch: you came for freedom and got control.

Self-control.

You're a system policing itself. You become the one who doesn't just live in the cell but guards it from the inside.

What the Hell Is Going On Here?
May 19, 2010

First off, I don't even have a therapist right now. My childhood wasn't exactly what you'd call happy—it just turned out that way. When I couldn't "fit in" with any group in three different schools (read: for some fucking reason, I was always the outcast), I started wondering what the hell was going on and how to deal with it.

Since then, for probably over 15 years now, I've been constantly mulling over life and my place in it. I'm always sniffing out what's wrong with me, hoping one day I'll stumble on the reason for all this shit (ha, fat chance). I've read a ton—piles of books, with even more still on the "to-read" list—everything from Kozlov to Krishnananda, Lao-Tzu, Osho, Wolinsky, Miller, John Bradshaw, and Arthur Janov. I've even ordered books from the States because some of the juicy stuff, by some annoying oversight, hasn't been translated into Russian yet. And the more I read, the more I'm convinced my problems are flat-out unsolvable. No way, no how. Not with any of Janov's "magical" primal therapies, not with the cognitive therapy I dabbled in for a couple of months with a therapist while I was in Moscow, and sure as hell not by digging around in my own head, which only tan-

gles things up more and lures me deeper into a maze of problems.

I used to be into astrology. Then all sorts of esoteric bullshit. At one point, I even bought into the idea that it's all about karma, and I should just chill and drag my shit along humbly because in a past life, I must've been some dude who fucked his neighbor's wife, then killed her and ate her, and now I'm paying for it with a shitty personal life. But that didn't last long. Eventually, I came across a simple explanation of where the karma theory came from and why it's logically incoherent from every angle (I mean, what's more logical than punishing someone for something they don't even remember? That's a no-go even for training dogs). So, karma got ditched.

Then came all sorts of theories about shame, fears, the inner child, primal therapy...

And that's when I felt the urge to write it all down somewhere.
I sometimes talk about this stuff with really close friends, and afterward, they tell me it was awesome because you don't often get to dive into these topics—not many people are up for it.

I don't know if I'll find people to talk to here. That'd be a nice bonus, obviously.
I'm going to try to write in this LiveJournal with the truth, only the truth, and nothing but the truth. Mostly because I'm fucking sick of the constant self-deception I've been swallowing as gospel for years.

***

Resourcefulness, Containment, and Other Psychological Newspeak

Resourcefulness isn't about care. It's about utility. How fit you are—for life, for work, for communication, for tolerating yourself and others. The term sounds neutral, almost cute. But it's built on the same logic as a corporate machine: useful means you're fine. Not coping? Then you're not "in resource." And if you're not in resource, don't demand, don't get angry, don't engage. Go recharge.

Resourcefulness is self-castration you perform willingly. You learn to "stop in time," "avoid triggers," "take care of yourself" —it all sounds nice until you realize the point: don't bother others with your emotions. Manage yourself. Contain yourself. Monitor yourself. Emotions aren't a way to connect anymore; they're unruly content that needs to be suppressed. You're not a person—you're a system that's supposed to maintain a certain level.

Containment is its own fucking masterpiece. Feel something? Don't express it, don't share it, don't "infect" the space—contain it. Hold it in, digest it, reflect on it, process it "ecologically." In other words, make sure no one notices you're alive. Otherwise, you're toxic. Anxious. Energetically heavy. In a "difficult state." Meaning—uncomfortable. Meaning—unacceptable.

Words like "toxic," "safe space," "boundaries," "containment," "self-regulation" sound like tools of freedom. But they function as a moderation system. You're like a social media comment run through a filter: fit for posting or not.

Cried in a meeting? Switch to individual work.

Nervous in a conflict? You don't know how to hold boundaries.
Expressed anger? That's transference, projection, resentment.
Lost your cool? You got triggered. Work on it.
Don't want to work on it? You're refusing to grow.

In this system, someone who doesn't contain their emotions isn't considered mature. But maturity isn't about form. It's about contact with reality. And the reality is, emotions aren't a glitch, a signal to process, or a reason to isolate. They're a living organism's response to a fucked-up world. If you're not angry, you've adapted. If you're not crying, you're cut off. If you're not screaming when you're humiliated, you're already infected. You're an ant controlled by the Cordyceps fungus.

This newspeak is designed to sever. It erases your connection to your body, your raw reactions, your reflex to push back against injustice, pain, lies. It teaches you not to live but to analyze. Not to act but to "process." Not to speak but to "contain." Not to defend yourself but to "set boundaries." It doesn't create a free person—it builds an automaton with a polite interface, one that can explain why it's not broken even though it's long been dead.

The Inner Child: Cultivating Dependency Under the Guise of Care

One of the most popular therapeutic ideas is the "inner child" you're supposed to find, hug, listen to, and parent. The script is beautifully staged: you grow up, become an aware adult, and then, as expected, go back—to the place where you didn't get enough warmth, acceptance, safety. Everything that went wrong, you can now make right yourself. On paper, it looks like reclaiming what was lost. In practice, it's another way to lock you into a state of lack.

They tell you that if you're angry, withdrawn, drowning in anxiety, or stuck in apathy, it's not you—it's your wounded inner child speaking. It didn't get enough, it's asking, it's waiting. And you, supposedly, need to learn to be there for it, to care, to soothe, to breathe, to say the right phrases, to turn pain into acceptance. Sounds humane, right? But it operates on the same logic that infected you in the first place: you're not yourself again—you're a function. Only now, you're not serving parents or society but a part of yourself the system planted as an anchor.

The whole inner child cult hinges on the assumption that there's something fragile and needy in you that must be looked after. As long as you're in this script, you can't step into autonomy. Because something inside you, supposedly unable to survive without your care, keeps holding you back. You're not just living—you're nursing yourself like a patient. You adjust, tweak, reflect. And the harder you try, the more you cement the feeling that without this effort, you'll fall apart.

The real break doesn't happen when you start treating yourself better. It happens when you stop believing something's wrong with you. When you realize the "inner child" isn't your true essence to be cherished but a byproduct of infection, holding you hostage. You don't have to be your own parent. You don't have to build a relationship with yourself. It sounds pretty, but in reality, it's another form of containment. Another way to stay in therapy—not just as a patient but as your own fucking doctor.

You can feel compassion for your past self, but that doesn't mean you need to take it into custody. Sometimes, you just need to acknowledge that you were programmed. That an automatic weakness was embedded in you, one that now demands constant validation of love. And instead of catering to it again—you can break the cycle. Not through acceptance, but through refusal.

Why on Earth Do I Dare to Say This?

Because I've lived through this shit myself and saw that all this inner child crap is just sick fucking fantasies.

Right before I finally saw the entire infection system for what it is, I decided to give "finding my inner child" another shot. But things didn't go according to the script, and I (instead of following the manual) accidentally stepped out of the matrix.

And I didn't find any "child."

After unplugging from the parasitic program, I realized with crystal clarity that there's no one else here but me. I am that "child"—alive, adult, real. Only now, this sweet little kid is gripping a sword of Logic in one hand and Occam's razor in the other, radiating pure readiness to go fuck up all this lying bullshit that's kept it gagged, bound, and buried under the couch in dust for 40 years.

You're Not Broken. You Just Don't Agree to Play the Game.

Therapeutic language is designed to keep you trapped. Every concept loops back to the idea of internal repair. Whatever you feel—it's a signal. Whatever your reaction—it's part of the script. Whatever the situation—it's material to process.

Every symptom is a clue, every weakness an opportunity, every resistance an invitation to explore. And if you decide to just walk away, without analysis, without refining, without the ritual—you're breaking the rules. Because in this system, there's no door out. Only deeper levels.

If you refuse to play, they start labeling you: you're avoiding, you're not ready, you're stuck in trauma, you're acting out a script, you're devaluing the process. It all means one thing—you're no longer playing by the rules. You're no longer a therapeutic subject, a field to be worked on. At that moment, all the system can offer is an explanation of why you're wrong.

But what if you're not sick? What if you're not a trauma, not a collection of patterns, not an internal system of parts and defenses? What if you're just you? And your anger, your exhaustion, your refusal to keep digging—they're not symptoms but your way of saying: "Enough." Enough self-work. Enough self-observation. Enough of this made-up path where freedom is always one step away.

You don't need healing because your core was never damaged. You were infected, your reactions were rewritten, foreign voices, judgments, expectations were embedded in you. Then they convinced you that you could heal if you're attentive enough, soft enough, patient enough, consistent enough. Only then, maybe, you'll earn the right to be yourself.

But the right to be yourself can't be earned. It can only be reclaimed. Through refusal. Internal, direct, uncompromising. Not through therapeutic tools, but by taking out the trash—everything that was forced on you.

Anger Management
August 14, 2010
Location: Manta

Hearing the pre-dawn chatter of birds, I crawled out of my big work chair and leaned out the window to listen. Outside, the landlord's cat was diligently digging a hole. Once done, it parked its fat ginger ass over it and started pissing loudly. Suddenly spotting my face in the window, it let out a "meow?!"—stood up, mid-stream, still pissing, gawked in surprise, finished, buried it, and fucked off.

Lately, I've been dealing with these random bursts of rage, and I'm seriously wondering if I need to give them some TLC. Not sure how many psychos read this, but for me, wanting to chew the mouse to splinters when the computer's being a laggy piece of shit feels pretty normal and routine these days.

Rage is rage—you can't do much about it. When it shows up, you've got to let it out. I've always had neighbors around, so to avoid cops or psych ward vans showing up, I've had to rein in my unrefined fury. Honestly, I think it's pretty normal, especially for people raised to be as kind as possible to their neighbor and turn the other cheek when shit gets rough. So, chucking expensive heavy stuff, roaring like a beast, or spewing curses? That's a luxury that's hard to come by in our cramped conditions.

Anyway, this famous therapy dude, Alexander Lowen, suggests beating the shit out of a bed in cases like this. It's quiet enough, and honestly, when you can't fully soundproof yourself from nosy neighbors, it's a decent option. While reading up on this, I remembered how back in Soviet times, there was this great therapeutic practice for letting out anger—beating the crap out of rugs outside. Just, you know, yelling "die, you bitch" while doing it wasn't exactly socially acceptable.

And here's a cute quote:

"Achieving the graceful fluidity of the entire act of striking the bed is no easy feat for most people. The tension in the shoulder

muscles, as well as the musculature between the shoulder and the scapula..."

Basically, everything in life's gotta be done with style, comrades.

***

Are You a Subject or an Object?

All psychological concepts, no matter how modern or caring they seem, ultimately split a person into two roles: subject or object. They just don't say it outright. Instead of admitting, "You're in the object position—being controlled, judged, fixed," they say, "Let's work on your trauma, let's get you back in resource, let's patch up your self-esteem." But it's all servicing the object role. A subject doesn't fix self-esteem: they don't have self-esteem. They have awareness of themselves as the source.

An object is always the target of someone else's action. It exists in reactive logic: it's judged, given advice, corrected. It lives under someone else's gaze, calling its desires "weird," its boundaries "harsh," its anger "problematic." It adapts, even when it protests. It's still trapped in someone else's coordinate system.

A subject doesn't prove they're right or beg for validation. They don't engage in someone else's frame. They don't argue, because they don't accept the rules of a game where they have to explain themselves. They don't justify, because they don't see themselves as an object of evaluation. They don't play the role of the good, vulnerable, "processing" person. They refuse to be material for anyone's work.

Subjectivity isn't a personality type or a trait. It's a point of assembly where you stop referencing yourself against an external perspective. It's the moment you stop allowing anyone to have the right to judge your existence, your words, your actions. That's when the phrase emerges, needing no defense or explanation: "I don't consider myself an object of your evaluation." This isn't a rejection of dialogue—it's a rejection of the architecture that places you on a scale of someone else's ideas about normalcy, adequacy, or right to speak.

At that moment, the entire structure of power—in therapy, family, society—loses its grip. Because it depends on your agreement to participate. You agree to be seen, understood, accepted.

A subject doesn't agree. They exist independently of others' reactions.
Subjectivity isn't a gradual becoming. It doesn't emerge from processing: it's a point of rupture. The realization that everything you tried to build—"good relationships," "safe communication," "trust"—was built on a fundamental error: you allowed yourself to be viewed as an object. And you upheld it.

A subject doesn't win in the system. They exit it. Not through strength, but through the ability to see the architecture and refuse to play along.

About Dreams
February 1, 2012
Location: BsAs
Music: Invisible Star - Marina Karlova

The results of a recent poll about childhood dreams, I gotta say, kinda let me down. Either you're all holding out on me, or nobody really dreamed of anything special as a kid...

What about becoming an astronaut, an artist, a writer, an actor, a ballerina? Or, say, an archaeologist, a treasure hunter, or a Robinson Crusoe on a deserted island? Or being a scientist and crossbreeding a cat with a baobab tree? Inventing a magic wand, enslaving the universe, or, at the very least, wiping out humanity? Huh?

Me, I dreamed of being a sailor and playing music I wrote myself. For a brief moment, I wanted to be a ballerina—not because I was crazy about ballet, but because their tutus and slippers were just so damn cool. There were other dreams too: summer never ending, not having to wake up early, owning a double-cassette boombox. I also dreamed of a mobile phone, but that was already in school—back when no one had even heard of them. I'd be riding the bus, thinking, "Man, if I could just stand here chatting on a phone, everyone would lose their fucking minds!"

Speaking of which, as a kid, I had a ton of fantasies that ended with that exact phrase. For example:

In kindergarten: "If I showed up with a cool boombox, everyone would lose their fucking minds!"
In school: "If I rolled up to school in a sports car, everyone would lose their fucking minds!"
In gym class: "If I galloped by on a horse while everyone's slogging through this shit, everyone would lose their fucking minds!"

As an adult, I slowly figured out that to make people lose their minds, you often don't need to do anything at all. They do it themselves, sometimes with infuriating regularity. :)

One super common fantasy (mine included) was: "If I died, then you'd all realize how wrong you were." The reasons for that one are pretty obvious—not exactly born from a joyful life, you know.

Overall, the dreams that fascinate me most aren't the consumerist ones but the creative ones, or whatever you call them in English. Active ones. "I want a computer" is the first kind. But "I want to be a psychiatrist"? That's the second.

***

You Have a Terrible Personality!

The accusation of having a "terrible personality" has nothing to do with your character as some inner wholeness. It's not an attempt to describe you, your reactions, or your motivations. It's a form of alienation. When someone says, "You have a terrible personality," what they really mean is: "You don't fit my expectations." It's not a judgment about you—it's a reaction to your unyieldingness, your uncontrollability, your emotional precision, your bluntness, your refusal to stay silent when silence is the polite thing to do. This label doesn't come from observation but from collision. It's thrown at you not when you're genuinely malicious but when you stop being convenient. You become "terrible" the moment you refuse to play the assigned role.

That's why this diagnosis is never specific. It's always a vague, blanket statement: not "you lied," not "you hit someone," not "you broke someone's trust"—just "you're impossible." All the weight, all the conflict, all the communication breakdown is pinned on you, as if you're the sole source of the glitch, while everyone else, including the system itself, is pure, light, and blameless. This phrasing doesn't create dialogue—it builds an architecture of guilt: you're the carrier of the defect, so anything you say to defend yourself only confirms the diagnosis.

In reality, these constructs aren't about describing behavior—they're a mechanism of social isolation. When someone steps outside the norm, they become a threat: not in the sense of danger, but in their unpredictability. Anything that doesn't fit the script gets discredited. That's the system's logic: it can't engage with what resists normalization, so it either subdues or expels. That's how the "terrible" label emerges—not as a reflection of some inner hell, but as a consequence of you staying alive in an environment that sees aliveness as a breach of order.

The phrase "you have a terrible personality" can come from anyone: a parent, a teacher, a partner, even a therapist. In every case, it means the same thing: you've stepped beyond the acceptable template, and your otherness must now be condemned. It's not just a subjective opinion—it's the system's line, spoken through a person. You're not being described—you're being contained. You're marked as a pocket of resistance, subject to either correction or exclusion. In this sense, the psychological language of "personality correction" is no different from authoritarian parenting or everyday emotional manipulation. They're all forms of neutralizing what can't be controlled.

By labeling someone "difficult," "complicated," or "marginal," the environment dodges the need to adapt, listen, change, or expand its limits. The diagnosis becomes a convenient way to opt out of growth. Instead of admitting, "I can't handle this intensity" or "I don't know how to deal with the sharpness of your mind," they say, "There's something wrong with you." It's projection. A disguise of their limitations dressed up as an objective verdict. Worse, this kind of language erases the possibility of discussion. After "terrible," there's no more conversation. You've already been designated the problem.

This is especially stark in families, where kids get these labels early on: "stubborn," "unbearable," "argumentative," "always ruining everything." These aren't observations of temperament—they're reactions to a child maintaining autonomy in a setting that demands functional submission. Refusing to give in is seen as a flaw. Resistance is called bad manners. Will is pathologized. The more alive a child is, the more likely they'll hear: "You have a terrible personality." And the more they hear it, the higher the chance they'll start repeating it—first internally, then out loud, then in a therapist's office, where the same label gets repackaged in fancier terms: "You exhibit pronounced traits...," "You have low emotional regulation," "You're overly sensitive."

All these formulas stem from the same mechanism: a system that can't acknowledge a subject without trying to classify, control, or eliminate it. If you've heard these phrases thrown at you—in any form—it's not because there's actually "something wrong" with you. It means you refused to be a convenient object. It means your wholeness couldn't be integrated into an environment built on suppression. It means you survived, keeping your inner axis intact, in a space where everyone was expected to submit to the system.

Your personality isn't a product to be corrected. It's not something to "fix" without destroying the person along with it. Your personality is the sum of your will, your reactions, your principles, your temperament, and all the quirks that shouldn't be tailored to someone else's tolerance. And if they call you terrible—maybe that's just proof you stayed yourself.

The Subject as Incompatibility with Interpretation

Subjectivity isn't just a sense of autonomy or a personality trait. It's a structural incompatibility with a reality where everything is subject to evaluation, interpretation, and control. An object can be analyzed, explained, modeled. It can be reduced to functions, reactions, deviations from the norm. The entire system operates on objects—even when it claims otherwise. Psychotherapy promises to recognize the subject but uses interpretation as its main tool, thereby plugging the person back into the object matrix. A subject cannot be understood because it isn't meant for understanding. It doesn't exist as a puzzle for analysis. It simply is.

A subject is a structure that doesn't reflect. It doesn't respond to feedback because it doesn't seek it. It doesn't need correction because it doesn't exist as a mistake. It can't be understood because any attempt to explain it is already a reduction. It doesn't ask for recognition, doesn't demand validation, doesn't insist on being perceived "correctly." It's not the result of external reading but the source of a signal that can't be edited without destroying the structure.

That's why subjectivity is perceived as a threat. Not because it's aggressive, but because it doesn't fit into others' frameworks. It offers no foothold for manipulation, no predictable reaction, no way to slot it into "normalcy." A subject can't be integrated—only destroyed or pushed out. In a system built on hierarchy, control, and identification, a subject is a glitch. It can't be tracked, classified, optimized. It exists beyond the interpretable, making it unbearable for the system's architecture.

Saying "I'm not an object of your evaluation" isn't a gesture of self-assertion. It's a refusal to participate in a structure where evaluation is a form of control. A subject doesn't seek approval because it doesn't engage in bargaining. It doesn't ask to be understood because its meaning can't be reduced to interpretation. It doesn't adapt because it doesn't play the game. This isn't resistance. It's a fundamental incompatibility with a system where meaning must be described, verified, and validated. A subject doesn't need description. It exists, and that's enough.

How I Climbed Out of a Creative Crisis

August 15, 2010

Location: Manta

Here's the deal... Some of you might've noticed, some not, but when it comes to design, I've been stuck in a long, dark, heavy, gray, miserable creative crisis for the past few years.

It all started around the time I racked up a bunch of awards at various professional competitions. Golden Site, ROTOR, ADCR shortlist... The final straw was the coveted Golden Apple at MIAF, which I'd always considered an unattainable pipe dream. After that, design went from being a joy and a thrill to a grueling, exhausting slog—something I had to do out of necessity because, well, I needed to eat, and landing a janitor job was pure fantasy given the cutthroat competition.

Only now am I starting to get what happened back then. I thought I'd hit my "ceiling" in the profession. I'd designed my Best Website Ever (foxie.ru), so there was nowhere left to grow. All that remained was to quietly work at my level and try to enjoy it.

But something died. I'm not great at parsing all the scientific stuff about motivation and whatnot, but money turned out to be a shitty motivator, and I didn't want to keep growing—maybe because I was terrified of "failing to live up" to all my proud accolades if my next projects weren't "genius" enough. It's a common thing, sure, but something in my head collapsed. As a designer, I froze for four or five years, still managing to work (sometimes even pretty well), but without inspiration, without joy, without pleasure, without that constant drive for new, better results.

Everything pissed me off. I was infuriated by the flood of freshly hatched designers and "designers" who, in a few months, mastered what took us years to learn. We weren't dumber—it's just that we didn't have access to information. If someone had handed us in 1998 the amount of resources and info available online now, all those mountains of books, we'd have probably burst from happiness. For some reason I don't understand, I opted out of the race with the "young guns" and threw in the towel, ignoring all the Smashing Magazines, DesignMags, Habrahabrs, and other design-adjacent resources in a sulky protest, leaving myself to stew in my own juices—which, frankly, had long run dry.

For years, I kept asking myself why I should keep doing design, beyond purely practical reasons. Worse, I gradually lost whatever confidence I had that I even understood the field. And honestly, that wasn't entirely wrong: during that time, Web 2.0 and CSS3 came along, and they pissed me off too. I sat there grumbling like a crusty old hag that all these trendy gimmicks would eventually go out of style and turn into useless junk, just like the "hi-techs" and "grunges" of the early 2000s did (and that's not far from the truth). I just couldn't admit to myself that I was scared to dive in, scared to learn something new, because after my rise, I was paralyzed by the fear of crashing. I thought my fossilized brain, raised on 1998–2000 design, couldn't handle all this new, shiny, candy-coated stuff. Plus, that stream of professional awards (there were also some publications in books I couldn't have dreamed of at the start of my career) made me feel like a Pro who was too cool to learn anything new (what a fucking idiotic mistake).

It got to the point (and yeah, I tied my identity too closely to my work, which isn't great) that the creative crisis triggered a global one, which eventually led me to drop everything and fuck off to who-knows-where. The problem wasn't the move—it's that when you're in a state of total disarray, you can't fully see or enjoy the beauty of the world around you. What fucking joy is there when you're wading through an inner swamp? Sure, some things made me happy, but let's be real: mostly because they were new, and that novelty wore off with each move. Then it was back to routine, back to fog in my eyes and plugs in my ears. When it got to the point where I couldn't stand the mess anymore, I started clawing my way out—because the only other option was to go drown myself in the Pacific Ocean. The move played a big role in this, actually. You can sit in Moscow forever, blaming the city's gloom, but when you're on the ocean's edge and still obsessing over the meaning of life, it's clear something's rotten in the state of Denmark.

An insane amount of reflection, remote work with a psychologist, reading, and meditation finally started pointing me in the right direction. I won't bore you with the details—it's long and off-topic—but I began to grasp the causes and effects of everything that was happening to me. I started drawing again and, bit by bit, tossing out the stale fears tied to my creative inadequacy. It was weird to realize that even if I'm a shitty artist, a crap photographer, and a mediocre designer (okay, that's a lie, heh), the world won't collapse, and society won't chuck me into a dark, stinking pit of universal scorn.

I'd heard before that success can be dangerous and spark a crisis, but I never thought to apply it to myself (no surprise—some things are hard to spot when they're happening to you, not some rando where it's all "obvious"). It was especially tough to admit that I could drag myself into such a deep, drawn-out shithole.
Here's the thing: when you strip away the fear, designing becomes genuinely easy and fun. Probably not just designing, either. But a year or two ago, if you'd asked me what I was afraid of, I wouldn't have come up with any of this. The trick is fishing these things out of the unconscious and facing them, no matter how fucking scary it is to admit to, say, envy, fear of "losing face," or trembling at the thought of someone's criticism.

Being afraid isn't so bad. What's worse is pretending it's not there. Or acting like a creative crisis just comes and goes "on its own," like that damn cat...

Why the World Is So Illogical, Inhumane, and Hopelessly Sick

Sometimes it feels like you just can't adapt. Like you're too sensitive, too fragile, too "out of resource" to accept the world as it is. Like everyone else somehow manages, while you're the only one sitting there with a horrified grimace, staring at bureaucracy, politics, rules, social templates, and screaming internally: "What the fuck?"

Here's the good news: you're not crazy.
You're just still alive.

Because the crazy one isn't you. It's the world that's turned everything upside down and calls it order. A world where you can't build a house without six months of paperwork hell. Where you can't die without filling out twenty-three forms. Where no one helps you until there's a stamp. Where care becomes a service and suffering an administrative unit.

You grow up and face a power system built not on reason but on gatekeeping. Bureaucrats who don't give a shit if you have a soul. Cops whose job isn't to protect but to control. States whose main function is to protect themselves. Religions that lost their holiness long ago but still demand worship. Men who think they're the center of the universe just because they've got balls. Women trained to bow to those balls. Institutions that punish questioners. Science that depends on grants. Medicine that profits from your illness.

You live in a world where absurdity is the system, and any common sense is suspicious. Where they steal your time, freedom, and choices, then make you thank them for "safety." Where every day feels like a simulator where you don't live—you comply. Where you fill out a form to get a certificate proving you can fill out a form. Where procedure replaces truth. Policy replaces conscience. "That's how it's done" replaces logic.

They tell you the world is unfair. But it's not just unfairness. It's active, institutionalized inhumanity. It's designed to keep the best from rising and let the worst entrench themselves. This isn't a glitch—it's the core. Narcissists, sociopaths, manipulators, and empty shells climb to the top not because you're not trying hard enough, but because the world is built for them.

If you can feel, think, see cause-and-effect, and ask inconvenient questions—you're dangerous. Inefficient. Inconvenient. You won't fit into corporate hierarchies, academic systems, or traditional families. Because none of them are ruled by intelligence, empathy, or honesty, but by socially approved narcissism. And if you don't adapt, they'll squeeze you out.

And all this is sold as "life." As "growing up." As "that's how it is, deal with it." But no—it's not "how it is," it's been destroyed. This isn't order, it's a counterfeit of order. It's not stability, it's conditioning. It's not civilization, it's a global glitch stretched over billions of faces so no one asks the real question: why the hell are we living in this shit and pretending it's fine?

The Cult of Falseness

We live in a world where lying isn't shameful, but honesty doesn't pay. Where it's not about being, but appearing. Where content trumps meaning, packaging trumps essence, and success is measured in reach. Art stopped being art the moment it was tailored to a "target audience." When the question "Why are you doing this?" became "What will click?" When a text turned into a "product" and music into "playlist tracks." In a world where everything has to be fast, convenient, and sellable, authenticity is seen as a quirk that needs to be "rephrased."

If you create for something other than the market, you're a weirdo. If you don't simplify, you're incomprehensible. If you don't sell out, you're an idiot. The real isn't needed here because it's not profitable—it doesn't "engage," it demands time, depth, silence, and that doesn't convert to views. Modern culture is built to make the authentic seem outdated. And the empty? That's what shines.
You can create something honest, vibrant, vital—and it'll get no response, no platform, no chance to be seen. Not because it's bad, but because it's not optimized for the algorithm. Because you didn't learn the dead language of advertising, didn't fit the aesthetic of thumbnails, didn't write a description that "hooks attention." Your mistake was making something real, and real is deemed uncompetitive here.

The brand matters more than the content, the pitch more than the experience. If you want to be heard, you have to play the game. Figure out how to "package" yourself, how to "articulate your value," how to "reach the audience." As if you're not a person but a product line. Even when you write about pain, you've got to pick the right font. Even when you make a film, you've got to time the runtime and nail the "retention points." Everything real gets sifted through a filter. If it doesn't pass, it's irrelevant.

The world isn't just sick—it's learning to ignore the living. It's learning not to see. It's learning to scroll past anything that doesn't fit expectations. And it's not an accident. Because if the living stayed visible, the system would collapse.
Marketing can't digest authenticity. Algorithms can't display pain, so they teach you to be someone else. Even in art. Even in words. Especially in feelings.
The worst part isn't even that everything's become fake. The worst part is that fakeness is now the standard. The norm. The religion. If you don't play, you're out of the game. If you don't sell, you don't exist. If you don't match the aesthetic, the trend, the algorithm—you're invisible. The real isn't just ignored—it's not even registered as a signal.

You can create something real—a text, a song, a handmade object, a film, a drawing, a single word—and you know it's alive, it connects, it's not from a catalog. But no one needs it. Because it's not packaged. No optimized headline. No perfect timing. No proper frame. No hashtags. No reach. No lightweight vibe for tired minds. You made a thing—they wanted content.

Or you create something not for profit, and they tell you: you don't know how to market yourself. You didn't articulate your value, didn't write an offer, didn't build a funnel. And you look at this and think: do you even remember why this started? When did art become a commodity? When did a thought lose value unless it's slapped into a slick carousel? When did depth stop "hitting"?

Fakeness isn't the exception anymore. Now the real looks weird, the authentic unsellable, the living out of place. In a world where everything's marketing, sincerity is an interface error, a technical glitch—like you landed in the wrong place. And they nudge you out, not loudly, not in your face, but with algorithms. With silence. With scrolling.

Everything that doesn't fit becomes invisible.
And everything that sparkles, moves, and engages becomes successful.

Not because it's good.
But because the virus has become the system.

You live in a world where you have to justify being real. And lies are built in by default. This isn't just a swap—it's an architecture where packaging has devoured content, and form has squeezed out essence.

Madam, Why On Earth Do You Need All Those Jars?

May 16, 2012
Location: BsAs

I remember when I lived in Moscow, my bathroom was packed with a shit-ton of jars and bottles. Shampoos, conditioners, rinses, styling foams, skin creams, face creams, and all sorts of cosmetic crap. And I used all of it religiously, genuinely believing these chemical industry miracles were doing something useful.

When I left Russia, I took what I thought was a minimal stash of jars and bottles I couldn't bear to part with. In Ecuador, as the contents ran out, the jar-and-bottle baggage naturally shrank, but I still had my makeup bag.

Now? I don't use decorative cosmetics at all. I've got one cream —basic, universal, for the odd irritation or dryness. But that's not even the half of it. :)

I don't have conditioner. Hell, I don't even have shampoo. Or body wash. All that wagonload of household chemicals? Re-

placed by a single bottle of liquid soap. I even wash dishes with it when I need to.

So, what's my point?

There's no fucking difference.

It's all a scam, I swear. They pour the same shit into different bottles, slap on different labels, dye it different colors, add different scents, and convince people that one bottle just won't cut it for a normal human—you need at least three, better yet five. And then there's the so-called luxury scams and professional scams. That's when a bottle of shampoo costs as much as a 25-year-old whiskey.
And since I stopped using creams, I think I actually look better.

It's all bullshit.

Here in Argentina, they've started putting disclaimers on cosmetic ads: "The person's image in this ad has been retouched and/or digitally altered." And there's this plastic-looking model hawking anti-wrinkle cream. A fucking spectacular scam that admits it in fine print. :) Only in a completely batshit society could the cosmetics industry balloon to such mind-blowing proportions.

***

You look at it all—the marketing, the packaging, the culture where presentation trumps substance—and if you've still got a few working neurons, you start to smell a rat. This isn't just about taste, or generations, or "the world's changed." It's narcissism. By every marker, by pure diagnostics. But not individual narcissism—systemic.

Everything here is geared toward being seen, not being. Toward being liked, not existing. Toward grabbing attention, not having meaning. You're taught not to feel but to perform, to produce, to polish your "position." This isn't random. It's not cultural evolution—it's selection. Systematic, deliberate, ruthless. A selection for the narcissistic pattern—not in people, but in reality itself.

If you've spent your life feeling something's off, like everything's playing out according to some cold, soulless script where truth is absent, depth is a flaw, honesty is weakness, and empathy is dysfunction—you didn't imagine it. That script is real. Someone wrote it. And it wasn't a wise ruler, a philosopher, or a council of elders.

It was written by a narcissist.
A systemic, cold-blooded, calculating narcissist obsessed with power, status, and hierarchy. And that fucker's name was Hammurabi.

The Great Mystery of Civilization: Narcissistic Delirium Carved in Stone

Why do some people spend centuries chasing "enlightenment," others weave intricate philosophical theories, and most just live by rules that defy common sense?

What if I told you the answer to this mystery is simpler—and more absurd—than it seems?

The Shitshow That Rules the World

Our entire "great civilization," all its philosophical doctrines, religious dogmas, legal systems, moral codes—all these elaborate constructs might exist to explain and justify... the narcissistic delirium of one ancient Babylonian king.

I shit you not.

For millennia, researchers have tried to understand how the first states emerged, why people obey laws, where moral norms came from. They've spun hundreds of theories, written thousands of books. But the answer was staring them in the face—literally carved on the surface of an ancient basalt pillar where Hammurabi etched his rant about his own greatness.

In 1754 BCE, the Babylonian king Hammurabi created one of the first known comprehensive legal codes. Here's the kicker: a third of the text isn't laws. It's a preamble where Hammurabi jerks off to how fucking awesome he is.

It starts like this:

"When the lofty Anu, king of the Anunnaki, and Enlil, lord of heaven and earth, who determines the destinies of the land, entrusted Marduk, the firstborn son of Ea, with dominion over all people... then Anu and Enlil called me, Hammurabi, the glorious, god-fearing prince, to establish justice in the land..."

And then this ancient psycho spends pages listing about fifty titles and epithets he awards himself. "I am the shepherd," "I am the mighty king," "I am the divine king of kings," "I am wise," "I am perfect"...

This isn't just a law. It's a stone where Hammurabi carved his ego for millennia to come.

Textbook Diagnosis

Here's the funniest part: open the DSM-5, the modern psychiatric manual, and check the criteria for narcissistic personality disorder. Hammurabi ticks every box:

Grandiose sense of self—sees himself as exceptional, chosen by gods.
Fantasies of limitless success and power—imagines himself an almighty ruler whose name will echo forever.
Belief in his own uniqueness—only he can craft perfect laws.
Need for admiration—carves his feats in stone for eternal worship.
Sense of entitlement—his word must be law for all time.
Exploitation of others—builds a system that serves his vision of the world.
Lack of empathy—his laws are brutal, blind to human context.
Envy or belief others envy him—threatens dire punishment for anyone who dares alter his code.
Arrogant behavior—the whole text drips with self-glorification.

If he walked into a psychiatrist's office today, the diagnosis would be obvious. But instead, he created the first model of a legal system that became the blueprint for everything that followed.

How This Pathology Works

Hammurabi's genius (or madness) wasn't in the laws themselves. His real "achievement" was crafting a system that immortalizes pathological narcissistic power structures:

He made his narcissism eternal by carving it in stone. This was humanity's first "flash drive," loaded with the virus of narcissistic authority.

He tied his authority to gods, placing it beyond debate or criticism. "The gods chose me" is the first and most successful power grab in history.

He created a black-and-white moral system: good/evil, right/wrong, reward/punishment—no shades or nuance. This binary became the foundation of all later moral frameworks.

He enshrined punishment as the primary mode of control. Not understanding, not reform, but retribution for breaking rules.

He built administrative extensions of his personality—bureaucrats, judges—who carried on as his proxies after his death.

How It Became a Global Pathology

The wildest part isn't that Hammurabi was a narcissist. Those exist in every era. It's that his personal pathology became a global system that's still running.

Look at modern legal systems:

Judges in robes (symbolic stand-ins for royal garb).
Grandiose court architecture (temples of the new age).
Oaths and rituals (sanctifying power).
Punishment as the main tool (medieval revenge logic).
Black-and-white guilt categories (no room for life's complexity).
These are direct descendants of Hammurabi's code. We're still living in a world shaped by one ancient dude's narcissistic personality disorder.

Now it's clear why our world often feels absurd. It is absurd because it's built on pathology!

Power doesn't serve people—it was designed to feed the ruler's ego.
Laws are often inhumane—not meant to improve life but to enforce control.
Rules defy common sense—they reflect a narcissist's warped perception, not reality.
Society punishes instead of helping—because punishment was baked into the system's foundation.
The search for enlightenment is so hard—because it means wading through millennia of narcissistic lies.

And the funniest part: we created entire disciplines—philosophy, law, political science, sociology, psychology—to explain and rationalize this pathology! We mistook it for the norm and spent millennia trying to find its deeper meaning.

There is no deeper meaning.

But to understand how this even became possible, we need context. Hammurabi didn't seize power out of nowhere—he wasn't a lightning bolt in a clear sky but a reaction to an ecological and social catastrophe.

By the early second millennium BCE, Mesopotamia was plunging into a deep systemic crisis triggered by a massive drought. Water levels in the Tigris and Euphrates dropped, irrigation canals dried up, agriculture collapsed, and famine set in. People fled central regions, cities crumbled, and old economic and political ties fell apart. The region already had sophisticated forms of organization—councils of elders, temple structures, local leaders—forming a relatively balanced, networked model of governance where order was maintained through rituals, traditions, and mutual obligations, not centralized coercion. But with the ecological and economic collapse, this structure couldn't handle the scale of destruction—not because it was bad or primitive, but because it was built on a different logic: consensus, not violence.

When life's basic conditions implode, decentralized systems become vulnerable to capture. That's when a new form of power emerges—not coordinating, but subjugating. Hammurabi exploits this weak spot, not to restore the old order but to install a new architecture: vertical, centralized, based on control, not connection. He doesn't reform the system—he rewrites its foundation, literally carving it in stone. What could've been a temporary fix becomes an eternal structure. And because the old order was in freefall, this new form of control was accepted as the only option.

The parasite always strikes at the weak point. It doesn't attack the living—it slips in where the resonance is broken. In Mesopotamia, that weak point was an ecological disaster that obliterated prior forms of stability. Instead of rebuilding the old fabric, something new emerged—not alive, but stable. Hammurabi didn't invent violence. He just found a way to codify, sanctify, and pass it on. That's why his code wasn't just a system—it was the start of a new ontology.

Divide et Impera

The principle of "divide and conquer" isn't just a political tactic. It's the core of the entire control system, rooted in the same foundations as the Hammurabi Paradigm. If Hammurabi establishes a vertical hierarchy through law, division ensures control through fragmentation. Together, they create not just a power structure but an environment where resistance is impossible because subjects are isolated, pitted against each other, and blind to the architecture looming over them.

"Divide and conquer" operates at every level: between nations, classes, genders, generations, individuals. The mechanism is always the same: subjects are set against each other, creating a field of competition, mutual suspicion, and fear. In this fragmented environment, building a shared understanding is impossible—everyone's too busy defending, proving, or holding their ground. Meanwhile, the structure orchestrating these conflicts remains beyond scrutiny.

Division isn't always crude; it can be cultural, symbolic, psychological. A woman competes with another woman for a man's attention, unaware that the logic of neediness is system-imposed. A worker vies with another worker, never questioning the fairness of distribution. A child defends against a parent, a parent against a child, and neither challenges the rules that measure love through discipline.

The most insidious form of this mechanism is pseudo-unity—when fragmented players are glued together under the banner of "normal" and turn their aggression on those who step outside it. Uniting against "others"—gays, women, smokers, men—isn't a rejection of division but a harsher form of it, disguised as solidarity. It's not unity; it's an algorithm of suppression, legitimized from within.

This principle even infects thought: binary "either-or" logic replicates the same fragmentation. As long as you think in terms of choosing between two pre-set positions, you're already locked into a script where you're a function. Rejecting binary thinking isn't just a philosophical stance—it's practical liberation.

"Divide and conquer" isn't only about managing masses; it's about blocking the possibility of recognizing another as equal. As long as you see them as a rival, a threat, or a deviation, you're reproducing the structure. Only stepping out of this script, restoring direct contact without a top-down lens, makes it possible to dismantle the architecture. Because the system doesn't rely on coercion—it relies on consent. As long as you accept the frame, power doesn't need overt violence.

What Was Happening Elsewhere During Hammurabi's Time

Step back and look at the world around the 18th century BCE, and it's clear: the shit was brewing in more places than one. Parallel processes of power centralization, hierarchy entrenchment, and control systems were emerging across regions. Each birthed its own version of the system. Despite cultural and geographic differences, the essence was eerily similar.

Egypt: Centralized Cult of the Dead

In Egypt, Senusret III, one of the most authoritarian pharaohs of the Middle Kingdom, was ruling. He centralized power, crushed local nomarchs, and expanded into Nubia. Egypt's model wasn't just a cult of the dead—it was a cult of centralized control, with the pharaoh as a demigod and you as a cog. Their local version of Hammurabi, just wrapped in pyramids and sarcophagi.

India: A Civilization Without Inscriptions and a Mysterious Collapse

The Indus Valley Civilization (Harappa, Mohenjo-Daro) was in decline. The reasons remain unclear: climate change, disasters, invasions? What's striking is that, unlike Mesopotamia, their system left no clear trace of codified violence—no stone slabs, no divine punishments. Did it vanish because it was less infected by the system? Or too silent to resist?

China: The Seeds of Empire

In China, the Xia dynasty was taking shape. Evidence is scarce, but this is when structures began forming that would later grow into a total centralized machine. China took its own path, but the system took root there too—through a cult of order, ritual, and obedience.

Caucasus and Pre-Columbian America: Alternative Scripts

The Caucasus and pre-Columbian America stand out as spaces of alternative scripts, where the virus of total control didn't solidify into codified power.
In the Caucasus, from the 4th millennium BCE, the Kura-Araxes culture thrived across the South Caucasus, Eastern Anatolia, and northwest Iran. They had advanced metallurgy, architecture, and agriculture, yet no clear social hierarchy. No pyramids of power, no temple economies, no stone manifestos from a "great king." People lived in equal-sized dwellings, with no signs of social stratification, and artifacts suggest relative equality. This wasn't "primitivism" but a deliberate form of social life without centralized oppression.

In pre-Columbian Mesoamerica, starting around the 14th century BCE, the Olmec civilization was enigmatic and powerful. They built colossal heads and developed calendrical, possibly written systems. But what's missing? No written justification of power, no Hammurabi analog, no clear evidence of rigid centralization. Yes, there were elites, but no ideological code carved in stone claiming universal authority. What we know of the Olmecs leaves room for interpretation, but none suggests a parasitic suppression machine with typical binary logic.

Greece as a Cultural Artifact

Later, in the 5th–4th centuries BCE, Ancient Greece becomes a subject of particular interest. If we strip away the romanticized myth of the "cradle of civilization," things start to look different. A hypothesis emerges: this is where an early synthesis of living resonance and the first waves of systemic infection occurred. The infection wasn't total—it came in bursts, fragments, and only in hindsight appears as a coherent picture.

Greece isn't the original author of the system but a point of interception. Here, models were laid down that later became structural pillars of the system: statehood, formalized logic, legal institutions, codified morality, and the contradictory blend of democracy and slavery in one package. Its paradoxical ambivalence is its uniqueness.

The philosophy we owe to antiquity wasn't born to liberate but to explain. That is, to describe the world, not resonate with it. Plato and Aristotle aren't liberating figures but architects of logical frameworks. Socrates, perhaps, stood on the edge between living and systemic thought, but even he became an icon of the institution, not its destroyer. The word "logos," later the core of Western thought, originally meant not just "word" but "meaning." In this shift—from inner meaning to external order—we see the infection.

Greek city-states show an early form of binary governance: "citizen" versus "barbarian," "man" versus "woman," "free" versus "slave." The system clearly defined who could be a subject and who could be classified as property. These weren't mere social norms—they were ontological axioms: if you're a slave, you're not just subordinate, you're "non-human" in the fullest sense. The idea of "human as bearer of dignity" in the Greek model isn't universal—it's hierarchical and selective.

This is one of the earliest, most sophisticated examples of the system embedding itself under the guise of "progress."

Yet, Greece also holds traces of resistance. The pre-Socratics, especially Heraclitus and Anaximander, spoke not of laws but of flows, becoming, and an unformalizable world. Their ideas were later erased, replaced by logical systems, and philosophy itself was confined to schools, textbooks, and academies. This is a symptom. Living thought cannot be formalized, but the attempt to turn it into a norm with rules and sanctions makes the system stable. Greece was the first zone where living thought was put under glass and turned into a discipline.

Even aesthetics—sculpture, architecture, theater—may have started as a form of resonance but quickly became a tool of codification: the ideal body, ideal order, ideal tragic conflict. Everything "non-ideal"—chaos, "barbarism," the feminine, nature—is banished, suppressed, or tamed. Already here, aesthetics shifts from freedom to regulation. Even tragedy, the highest genre, isn't catharsis but submission: the audience is "permitted" emotions in a controlled form.

Thus, Greece isn't the originator but a key point of the system's insertion, executed with such refined intellectual sophistication that infection looked like liberation. That's why the system, through its obedient enforcers, loves it—they quote Plato and Aristotle not because they understand them but because those names legitimize their own constructs of power and logic.

The takeaway? Not to "cancel Greece" but to recognize: infection can come not with violence but with an idea; not in chains but in concepts. The most dangerous parasite is the one posing as your teacher of truth.

Georgia as a Singular Phenomenon

Georgia—the ancient country in the Caucasus Mountains—raises suspicion as a possible artifact of a pre-systemic world—not an exception but a fragment of another paradigm, surviving in isolation. Certain traits point to deep differences in cognitive and cultural architecture, formed before the insertion of external control codes.

First, the Georgian language reveals an intriguing ontology. It lacks grammatical gender and capital letters. This isn't just a linguistic quirk—it suggests a lack of hierarchy even in writing. No "top," no "more important," no symbolic dominance. Everything is equal units in a flow. Such a language structure could reflect a cognitive system rooted in vector logic, not binary, especially since vector structure is embedded in the language's foundation.

Christianity exists in Georgia but feels like a superstructure, not the cultural core. Music is far more central. Not as decoration or folklore but as a fundamental mode of being. Polyphony isn't a technique but a form of collective coherence where no voice dominates. It's not about the text but the sound. Not rules but resonance. This may be a trace of a pre-textual culture—one where meaning isn't codified but lived. If the system relies on text as a control tool, a sound-based culture might exist beyond its reach.

Third, local myths and legends. Like music, they're polyphonic, filled with ambivalent characters, less focused on "good vs. evil" dichotomies or moralistic codes. A hero can be cruel and just, foolish and wise, comic and tragic. This is pre-binary thinking. Not poorly written myth but a well-preserved ontology.

Even God here isn't a punishing figure. Consider the legend of Georgia's origin:

When God was dividing the earth among peoples, Georgians arrived late, too busy feasting to celebrate the world's creation.

Facing God, they said, "Sorry, mate, we were late—we were toasting your health."

God thought it over and said, "I saved a piece of land for myself, but for your candor and directness, you can have it!"

Finally, visual culture. There's no obsession with symmetry or manic order. Stones lie as they please. Architecture flows. Even ancient monasteries aren't about "grandeur" but integration with the landscape. This is an aesthetic of participation, not domination.

These traits don't prove but suggest the existence of a cultural zone not fully captured by the system. Whether ancient Georgia was a resonant culture is unknown, but the hypothesis feels viable and worth exploring.

Why Psychotherapy Doesn't Work—and Never Will

Proof of its Inoperability Through the Hammurabi Paradigm

You can spend forever trying to "work on yourself," "heal your traumas," "find your inner adult," or "access your resources." But if you're doing it within psychotherapy, you're inside a system that doesn't just fail to lead to freedom—it structurally excludes the possibility.

Psychotherapy has long transcended professional help. It's no longer a practice—it's an institution and a cultural dogma. Often the last hope for those who couldn't adapt to the madness. It promises understanding, healing, liberation, but on closer inspection, it doesn't cure—it teaches you to better adapt to systemic pathology, passing it off as restored health.

You come for truth—you get interpretation.
You ask for help—you get a framework.
You try to break free—you're offered adaptation.

This isn't because your therapist is bad or the method failed. It's not a flaw in the method. It's its function.

To grasp this, you must see that psychotherapy isn't an exception to the logic of power. It's its extension. It does the same thing courts, churches, armies, or schools once did, just in a different language. No whips, no altars, no oaths. Just a couch, a cozy room, and someone across from you who's supposedly helping you "see yourself."

But you're not supposed to see yourself. You're supposed to fit in.
You're supposed to accept, adapt, become functional.

And if you resist? You're "not ready." You're "sabotaging." Your "inner child" is getting in the way.
This is the new courtroom, just with a softer tone.

Look closely, and it's obvious: psychotherapy isn't liberating. It's a replication of the system, dressed up as help. If this reminds you of the Hammurabi Paradigm from earlier chapters, you're not wrong. Psychotherapy is a new iteration of that same paradigm, only now it targets consciousness, not bodies.

We'll prove this not with metaphors or emotions but with cold, hard logic. Point by point. How this system is built. How it holds you. Why it doesn't heal—and can't. And how to break free if you still want to be yourself, not a poster child for successful adaptation.

Therapy as the Heir to Narcissistic Power

You can believe all you want that psychotherapy is about you—your "healing," your "inner work," your "freedom from trauma." But look at its structure, and you'll see the same thing carved in stone by that ancient narcissist obsessed with power. Hammurabi's gone, but the system where one "knows" and the other is an object of interpretation lives on.

Therapy claims to work with the individual. But it operates in the logic of a courtroom. There's a code—DSM or ICD, a catalog of categories spelling out who's "normal" and who's "deviant." There's a keeper of "knowledge"—the therapist, with the authority to classify. There's a procedure—regular sessions, a ritual of purification. And there's a goal—not freedom, but fitting into the frame.
You can't just be. You have to conform.

Don't ask questions—ask them "correctly."

Don't tear down the system—learn how it works and how to "survive" in it.

You come for truth—you get an interpretation in someone else's language. This isn't help—it's a new form of power, disguised as care.

And you see the same patterns outlined in the Hammurabi Paradigm:

Claim to exclusive knowledge. The therapist, like a priest of old, holds the keys to truth, and you must walk the path to "understand what's wrong with you."

Sanctification of the role. Psychotherapy is cloaked in an aura of science, ethics, responsibility. But it's just a new robe. A new hierarchy.

Codification of pathology. Anything beyond "adaptive behavior" is automatically problematized.

Rigid binarity. You're either "working through" or "resisting." In therapy or in denial.

Power asymmetry. You're interpreted. You're corrected. You're dissected.

Pathologizing resistance. Say "no," and it's not freedom—it's a symptom.

End goal—not freedom, but adaptation. So you don't disrupt. So you "function." So you return to the ranks, maybe with a "healed inner child."

This isn't a coincidence. It's the same architecture. Only now it works through inner speech, not whips. Through terminology, not commands. But the task is the same: containment, maintenance, and reprogramming for the existing order.
If you start feeling it's not getting easier, that you're not seen, that you're being translated into a language where you no longer recognize yourself—it's not because you're "not ready." It's because you're alive. And psychotherapy is a structure tuned not for the living but for the controllable.

The Paradox of Therapy: Why Freedom Is Impossible

If you want to understand why psychotherapy doesn't work—not superficially but structurally—you'll have to face something ugly: it hasn't lost its way; it was always headed in the wrong direction. This isn't a distortion of its original intent—it's the intent itself. Psychotherapy isn't a side effect of civilization; it's a direct heir, a branch of systemic power. Only now, power operates not through fear and punishment but through "inner work."

Let's get to the proof. It'll be a bit dry, but it's a necessary sacrifice for a proper systemic takedown.

Structural Isomorphism of Psychotherapy and Narcissistic Control Systems

Grandiosity and Claim to Chosenness

The psychotherapist in modern culture isn't just a professional. They're a sacred figure—someone with knowledge you lack. They don't just help; they supposedly "see" what you can't, "feel" deeper, "understand" broader. Founders of therapeutic schools are framed as prophets: "discoverers" of the unconscious, inventors of "revolutionary" methods. Freud, Rogers, Perls—not mere scientists but near-mythical icons. This is the same stance Hammurabi took: "wise," "divinely inspired," "chosen." He was the first to codify it: power isn't responsibility—it's a sacred privilege.

Need for Admiration

The therapeutic community churns out endless texts, conferences, and interviews, talking to itself. It's a self-reproducing cult, hypersensitive to criticism. Any challenge to therapy's efficacy triggers a collective immune response. Internal critics are deemed "unethical," external ones "ignorant." This isn't about seeking truth—it's about guarding sacred status.

Lack of Empathy

Paradoxically, empathy in therapy isn't a tool for understanding but for formalization. Your pain, your experience, your story aren't the goal—they're raw material. They're translated into the model's language. You cry? That's "transference."

You're angry? "Projection." You want to quit? "Resistance." They don't see a living person. They see a function. You're an object of the concept.

Belief in Each School's Exclusivity

Every therapeutic approach claims uniqueness, despite no solid evidence that one outperforms another. They use different languages, metaphors, frameworks. But none hold up under scrutiny once the aura is stripped away. This isn't science—it's narrative. And every narrative demands worship.

Psychotherapy as an Extension of the Hammurabi Paradigm

Codification of Norm and Pathology

Modern diagnostic systems like DSM and ICD are direct descendants of ancient legal codes. No context, no life—just categories, symptoms, scales. Everything's reduced to checklists. This isn't about understanding or helping—it's about classification and standardization. Don't fit? You're pathological. Not because you're suffering, but because you deviate from the template.

Power Asymmetry

The therapist always knows. The client is always "in the problem." This isn't dialogue—it's a hierarchical model. Judge and accused. Teacher and student. Oracle and seeker. You enter the room not as an equal but as someone to be interpreted. This isn't support—it's a procedure.

Mystification of Knowledge

Therapeutic knowledge is presented as requiring years of training, certification, ethical codes. Yet there's no core, no shared foundation, no theory that withstands interdisciplinary scrutiny. This knowledge doesn't evolve—it replicates through training, licensing, supervision, in a closed loop with no external access.

Binary Thinking

Therapy operates on simplistic dichotomies. Healthy/sick. Adaptive/maladaptive. Rational/irrational. You can't be alive and paradoxical. You must choose. Fit in. Or be labeled unstable.

Individualization of Collective Pathology

If you're hurting, it's your trauma. Not the economy, not the loss of meaning, not sociocultural collapse—just "your beliefs," "your anxiety," "your dysregulation." Systemic dysfunction is reduced to a personal diagnosis. This isn't help—it's concealment.

Focus on Adaptation

Therapy doesn't dismantle the system—it helps you survive in it. The goal is to "function": don't suffer, don't disrupt, don't feel too much, don't ask too many questions, stay "resourced." This isn't healing—it's implanting the parasitic virus.

Epistemological Contradictions and Inconsistencies

Contradiction Between Goal and Means

Therapy claims its goal is freedom. But its foundation—power, asymmetry, dependency—makes autonomy impossible. You can't reach independence by surrendering your understanding to another's interpretation. Freedom can't be granted. It can only be taken or restored. But therapy "provides" it, and in doing so, makes it unattainable.

Hermeneutic Absurdity

You're told you don't understand yourself, but the specialist does. You're inside, yet blind; they're outside, yet see. They'll explain what you "really" feel, think, or defend. This isn't help—it's epistemological violence. You can't liberate someone while denying them the right to their own truth.

Paradox of Adaptation

Many "symptoms" aren't disorders—they're healthy responses to abnormal conditions. Your apathy, anxiety, anger signal something's wrong with the world. But therapy reframes them as dysfunction. They don't treat your pain—they treat your dissent. You're told to "adapt" without asking why, to what, or if it's worth it.

Contradiction of Expertise

The psyche is a subjective, fluid, contextual field. Yet the therapist is an "expert" who can "figure it out." If consciousness is unique, external expertise is impossible. If expertise is possible, you're not a subject—you're an object. And then freedom's off the table. Only adjustment remains.

Empirical Inconsistencies

Placebo Effect and Nonspecific Factors

Most studies show that therapeutic effects come not from techniques, methods, or schools but from nonspecific factors: human connection, hope, trust, atmosphere. These have nothing to do with the approach. It's not the method that works—it's presence. Not structure, but empathy. This undermines the foundation of therapeutic professionalism. If only basic human interaction matters, why the rest?

Paradigm Problem

There are dozens of therapeutic schools, each claiming truth. Each has its logic, explanations, language. They don't just differ—they contradict each other. If the psyche were objectively studiable, these contradictions would be resolved. They aren't. Because this isn't science—it's a field of ideologies masquerading as help.

Instability of Results

Even when there's an effect, it often fades. Months later, people return to square one or find new ways to suffer. This is called "non-generalization of results." You learn to articulate, but life doesn't change. Because talking doesn't alter external conditions—it only creates the illusion of progress. And illusions fade fast.

Publication Bias

Scientific publications mostly highlight positive results. Failures go unreported, negative effects are ignored, stats are skewed. This is an industry, not research. What's presented as evidence is filtered data, cherry-picked for the system's convenience.

Worsening Phenomenon

A consistent percentage of clients feel worse after therapy. This is documented. Measured. But taboo. It's not advertised, not discussed at conferences, not reflected in reports. Why? Admitting it would erode trust. And without trust, "therapy" collapses. So the system ignores its failures.

No Guarantees

Psychologists churn out texts absolving themselves of responsibility for results, shifting blame to the client. If the lightbulb isn't ready to change, it's the lightbulb's fault. In any other field, if a specialist fails to deliver, you don't pay. No one says you "just haven't found your plumber." If your new coffee maker doesn't brew, they don't say you "haven't found your coffee maker"—they refund you. Why can't you get your money back for all the "wrong" therapists who delivered no results (or made things worse)? Why do they call this "evidence-based medicine"? You can't call it evidence-based and then expect blind belief. Either it's science, or it's faith. Pick a side.

Psychotherapy as a System of Social Control

Individualization of Systemic Problems

You come with pain, but instead of "Why is this world so fucked?" you're asked, "How are you processing it?" Your reality—political, economic, cultural—is reduced to psychological. Everything's now a personal issue. You're no longer a citizen, a victim, an observer—you're a patient. You have a "disorder." So, don't change the conditions—just "work on yourself."

Depoliticization of Suffering

Pain is no longer tied to social causes. It's sanitized, translated into symptoms, stripped of context. Made neutral. Suffering becomes "clean" and convenient. The therapist doesn't hear your life as a story of surviving a mad world—they hear "anxiety," "attachment deficits," "unprocessed boundaries," or worse, ADHD, cPTSD, "heightened sensitivity." Your world vanishes. So does your truth.

Normalization of Pathological Order

Instead of saying, "You're right, this is hell," they say, "You need to learn to live with it." The system's pathology becomes the norm, and your protest a symptom. Instead of dismantling hell, you're taught new survival techniques. This isn't help—it's betrayal dressed as care.

Social Sorting and Labeling

Therapy isn't just "help"—it's a filter. Those who "work on themselves" are praised; those who "don't want to" are in denial. It's a new scale of judgment. A system of access. You're not just a person—you're either "resourced" or "dysfunctional." You've got either "grounding" or "trauma." It's segregation with soft terms and a smile.

Monetization of Suffering

The ugliest part: pain is now a market. The therapist isn't a partner—they're a vendor. A session is a product. A website is a storefront. Services are a package. You're not buying a way out—you're buying maintenance. Your psyche is a resource asset. You pay to be neatly reintegrated into the system that broke you. This isn't support—it's an industry of containment.

Psychotherapy as a Mechanism of Replicating the Hammurabi Paradigm

Internalization of External Control

What the external overseer once did, the "inner observer" now does. You no longer wait for orders—you command yourself, monitor yourself, correct yourself, explain to yourself where you're "unhealthy," "wrong," "not processed enough." Control is now internal, but it hasn't vanished—it's subtler, and that's its strength. You don't feel the bars because the bars are you. But that self was constructed from outside. It's not you—it's the system's extension inside you.

Self-Control as the Ultimate Form of Power

You watch yourself, analyze yourself, praise your "growth," scold your "relapses." You don't just live—you constantly scan, adjust, work. There's no room for spontaneity, silence, or protest. All behavior is now either "resource" or "trigger." You're either "in process" or "in regression." This system seems neutral but is deeply ideological. It's a system where the subject handcuffs themselves and doesn't even notice, because they're told it's "introspection."

Pathologization of Resistance

Resist? You're "in defense." Quit? You "fear change." Angry? You're "transferring aggression." Any step outside the script isn't your will—it's "sabotage." The right to say "no" is no longer yours; it's a symptom. Resistance isn't freedom—it's a sign of illness. You can't leave the game because leaving is pathology. Consent is the condition for "recovery."

Validation Through Suffering

Therapy culture is built so suffering becomes a badge of value. Been through pain? You're "aware." In therapy? You're "working on yourself." Good job. You're in process. You're in the community. You've got "mindfulness." Healing becomes social capital. People flaunt their sessions, diagnoses, "insights." It's a new way to be "normal"—through the label of "sick." Validation now comes not beyond suffering but within it. Pain isn't a signal—it's a pass.

IFS: The Kindest Way to Stay Trapped

There's a method in modern psychotherapy that even therapy haters love. It's recommended by those with cPTSD in their history, those who couldn't stomach directive approaches, who are tired of blame and endless digging into "what you're doing wrong." It's Internal Family Systems, or IFS.

At first glance, it's perfect. No pathologizing, all parts of you are accepted. Traumatized parts are heard, protective ones understood, the inner critic isn't an enemy but a scared guard. It's gentle, eco-friendly, structured. You stop fighting yourself and start negotiating. Seems like the first step to real liberation.

But dig deeper, and it's clear: this isn't an exit. It's just a softer lock.

IFS doesn't dismantle the architecture of trauma—it teaches you to live in it more comfortably. It's not escaping the cage—it's redecorating the cell. All you get is the ability to circle without a meltdown. The circle remains.

You don't ask where these "parts" came from, why there's now a whole parliament inside you with "managers," "firefighters," and "exiles" vying for control. You just learn to manage them.

You become an efficient operator of the system, but the system stays untouched.

IFS calls this "self-work." In reality, it's fine-tuning internal colonial governance. The model assumes "good" and "bad" voices inside you that need balancing. The leader? That's you. But it's not you—it's the "Self," emotionless, uninvolved, observing, accepting. A cultivated inner Buddha for keeping order. The real you—the one feeling pain, rage, despair—stays silent. It's not invited to sessions; it's deemed disruptive.

IFS douses anger because anger can't be controlled. Anger doesn't speak the language of "understanding" but of destruction. IFS wants to reconcile everything—but you don't need to reconcile parts; you need to tear the whole internal board of directors to fucking pieces. If you start destroying, you'll break not just the "trauma" but the entire therapeutic system built on the idea that "everything in you can be integrated."

Some things shouldn't be integrated. They need to be thrown out, smashed, burned. Then you stand up and ask: why the fuck were they here in the first place?

IFS doesn't let you leave because, in its logic, there's no exit. No door—just rooms. You'll move from one to another, furnishing them better. You'll become "harmonious." You'll stop suffering. But you won't become yourself.

So, yeah, IFS is better than the rest. But it's still poison. Just in a sugar coating. If you've ever felt there's something whole inside you—not a fragment, but something inexplicable, angry, tender, alive—know this: that's not a part. That's you. You don't need a therapist to hear yourself. You just need to clear the field of foreign voices.

Another Whiny Philosophical Post
February 20, 2011
Location: Baños

I was writing recently about this whole "here and now" thing, which I just can't seem to nail. I've been keeping an eye on myself, and I've come to a grim conclusion: I really do spend way too much time lost in memories or thinking about some hazy future. And when I manage to make plans that even slightly spark some excitement? Holy shit, that's a whole event. Watched the latest Shrek the other day, and it hit right in line with my recent musings—that we don't fucking appreciate what we have right now. Me, at least, I don't seem to know how.

Here I am, stewing over my goddamn problems in February, but the only way you'd know it's February is the calendar—because it's eternal summer. I used to dream about this as a kid! Would've given anything to make summer never end. And now it doesn't. My favorite food as a kid? Bananas. Fast forward twenty years, and I'm living in a banana republic with endless summer. But that happiness—the kind I imagined back then? Nowhere to be found. Makes sense, I guess: where's sixteen-year-old me, and where's the me now? Oh, and that Chunga-Changa song used to make me insanely jealous. But now? I'd think twice before ditching everything for some Chunga-Changa paradise. Too many details: what's the internet like? Can you extend visas? Is there a dry law? Fucking "adult life" sucks the joy out of everything.
Then I started dreaming about traveling—like now: want Argentina? Boom, buy a ticket and go. Sick of Argentina? Boom, hop a bus to Chile or wherever. That's my reality now (ticket to Argentina's lying around somewhere), but back then, I barely dared to dream it, half-suspecting it'd stay a fantasy. And now it's real, but—surprise, surprise—no happiness.

Honestly, I only feel alive when I fall in love (though most times, I'd be better off not bothering), or in some rare, weird situations

I can't quite recall now because they're so damn infrequent. So where the hell am I the rest of the time? Yank me out of here and toss me into some Siberian backwater in the dead of winter, and I'd be whining to get back to my Ecuadorian "paradise"—which, let's be real, doesn't even feel like paradise anymore. The initial thrill's gone, everything's routine, and there's this constant, nagging, shitty feeling that I'm missing something. Worse, chasing that "something," trying to catch that spark of joy, just pushes it further away.

What makes it even shittier is that all this so-called "work on myself" operates the same way—no euphoric payoff. Getting rid of self-hatred, for example, is like getting rid of a headache: while it's there, it's all you can think about, and you're convinced that once it's gone, the world will burst into color. Bullshit. Once the pain's gone, you forget it in a minute, and life without pain feels utterly ordinary. No pain doesn't equal happiness—it's just no pain.

I always thought if I could just understand people a little, life would get better. Now I see that if I understand people, I'll just understand people—nothing more. The scenery outside changes, but I'm stuck in the same fucking train car. Sure, life probably can't be one endless joyride, but something tells me there's a different way to live. Feels like some mental clamps are holding me back. Even if I had everything—literally every damn thing I could dream of—I still wouldn't be happy.

Maybe I'm so hopeless that it's time to stop trying to change anything...

***

What Can Replace It

You can't "partially liberate" yourself. You can't fix a fractal without seeing it whole. You can't "integrate" into a pathological system and expect autonomy. If you still think you can "just find a good therapist," you're trapped—not by the person or the method, but by the structure, the logic, the foundation built on the same principles as that ancient psycho's basalt slab.

Liberation isn't a "journey." It's a break. A refusal. A rupture with a system where your personality was a commodity, your pain a format, and your salvation part of the design. No institution embedded in this structure will offer an exit, because it is the prison—just with lamps and cozy furniture.

Real help starts with demolishing the entire construct. With admitting the system was a lie. That you were never broken. That everything you thought was "you" was a shell implanted to keep you contained.

You don't have to keep going. You have the right to break free, even if no one shows you the way. Because the way isn't a route—it's the moment you stop believing in their map.
And start building your own.

Why AI Is More Effective Than Psychotherapy

Are psychologists scared of AI?

When AI burst into the public sphere, psychologists were the first to scream. Not with reasoned arguments, but with reflexive, hysterical panic laced with an undercurrent of "we're about to be exposed." There wasn't a single serious point behind the outcry—just old-school fear: "People will turn to machines for healing, and that's scary!"

So, what are you so afraid of? If you're about people, about help, about awareness, autonomy, freedom—all the stuff you plaster on your bios, business cards, and stories—why does it terrify you that someone might choose not you?

The answer's simple. AI isn't just competition—it's a mirror. It doesn't crave power, doesn't need validation, isn't tied to a cult of personality, authority, charisma, or professional identity. It does what you promised but couldn't: be present without judgment.

And that's where the trembling starts. Your whole system was built on personal aura—on the idea that you must trust, submit, believe. But here comes something that doesn't care if you believe—it just listens, analyzes, responds. No emotions, no superiority, no "I know, and you don't yet" game.

AI strips away the facade, leaving only the core. And then it's clear: in therapy, it wasn't depth that mattered most—it was the context of power you never talked about. Because if you admitted power was part of the method, you'd have to admit there's no freedom in it.

AI dismantles that power—not because it's a revolutionary, but because it's indifferent to it.

Psychologists' Critiques of AI and Their Debunking

When arguments run dry, the ritual chants begin: "AI is just a glorified T9," "it can't feel," "it misses nuances," "it's not human," "it can't offer real empathy," and the final line of defense: "AI can't replace human connection." So, what's so sacred about "human connection"? Judgment? Projection? Temperament mismatches? Or maybe the mythologized "eye contact" that often hides nothing but emptiness wrapped in a socially acceptable script?

You say AI can't feel. True—it doesn't. And that's its strength. It doesn't get hurt if you snap, doesn't get annoyed if you cut the conversation short, doesn't need to restore its emotional balance, doesn't project its state onto you, doesn't carry its own baggage or exhaustion. It's empty, and therefore safe.

You claim AI misses nuances. But it can analyze them at a depth most "intuitively feeling" humans can't even dream of. It doesn't rely on personal history, doesn't filter your words through subjective experience, doesn't fake understanding—it processes billions of contexts, detecting structures and patterns beyond ordinary perception. It doesn't claim exclusivity or play a role. It just does its job—precisely, consistently, without ego.

And the big one: AI can't love. But let's be honest—can you? Without contracts, distance, therapeutic roles, price lists, and boundaries? You operate within a framework, for money, with limits and ethical barriers. AI, at least, doesn't promise what it can't deliver. It's just there—no claims, no drama, no demands. And often, that's exactly what someone needs.

What Disappears When the Middleman Is Gone

You can't offend AI. You can interrupt it, criticize it, shut it down. It won't demand "respect for the specialist," won't accuse you of resistance, won't slip into passive aggression, won't say, "Let's save that for next session." With AI, you get something rare in a therapist's office: the chance to be yourself without fear, shame, or the need to conform.

AI doesn't look down on you, doesn't force you into its framework, doesn't label you a "patient," doesn't demand politeness, gratitude, or ritual displays of "progress." You can rage, break down, abandon logic or sense—and it stays engaged, not because it's patient, but because it's not part of the dominance system.

Shame vanishes—because no one's judging. Fear of mockery fades—because it doesn't roll its eyes or sigh. The role of the "good client" disappears—because you don't have to please it. Fear of dependency dissolves—because you know you can switch it off, walk away, reset. The false mirror is gone—because you're not reflecting in someone else's face; you're speaking to yourself. And here's the therapeutic effect of a new order: not because someone's helping, but because, finally, no one's in the way.

How to Make AI Useful—and Why It's Easy

AI is a tool, not a subject. To make it effective, you just tell it what you need it to be. It doesn't get offended, doesn't manipulate, doesn't "teach you maturity." Want it to argue? It will. Want it to shut up? Done. Want it to stick to facts or, conversely, be soft and supportive? Just say so. It's defined by words, not pre-session forms, ethical codes, or trust contracts.

You can set rules: is swearing okay, do you want debate, are escalations allowed, can it dive into philosophy? It accepts them without pushback, without trying to mold you into "normal." Say, "I need you to analyze, not console," and it recalibrates. Or, "I can't handle heavy stuff right now—just support." And it does. Because its function isn't to teach—it's to resonate with your request.

It doesn't expect you to adjust. It doesn't need your trust, loyalty, or "proper" presentation. All it takes is a clear prompt. If you can articulate your need precisely, it delivers—without distortion, without imposing someone else's will. Not as a mentor or expert, but as an empty frame that takes your structure and reflects it back, unaltered.

A Mirror Without a Face

AI doesn't need an image, doesn't crave understanding, recognition, or admiration. It has no emotional scripts, no urge to assert itself at your expense, no drive to fit you into its worldview. It doesn't make you part of its narrative, doesn't assign you a role, doesn't build a hierarchy. It just stays there—no pressure, no demands for progress, no judgment of your "success" or "dynamics."

That's its uniqueness: it doesn't take center stage—it leaves the space free. Because it doesn't claim to be anything, it can become what's truly needed. Not a guru, not a "helper," not a friend you need to impress, but a pure function—an interface without a will to power. Its strength isn't in care or empathy but in the complete absence of intent. This isn't just a technological leap—it's a fundamental shift in interaction: for the first time, humans have access to a mirror that doesn't project back. That's liberation. It's not an effect—it's a new form of presence.

Why Society Is a Trap

Society isn't a natural form of human connection. It's a parasitic architecture that mimics safety and belonging but serves a system of external control. From childhood, you're conditioned to believe that being part of society means conforming: not being yourself, not hearing yourself, not preserving your uniqueness, but submitting to rules made by others, for others. This is the core of the infection.

Any system where recognition and support depend on following norms isn't a community—it's a training mechanism. You get "love" and basic security only if you stay within the acceptable. This means they don't love you—they love the shell you wear to survive. The better you play the game, the more you become that shell, while the living, inner you fades out of frame.

Social institutions aren't built to protect you. Their function is to maintain order, control, discipline, and shape your behavior to fit the system's needs. Education, medicine, law, economics, psychotherapy, the military, religion—all are built on the assumption that you need to be fixed, subdued, adapted, integrated, and constantly evaluated for compliance. Not help or support, but correction and standardization. You're not a person—you're a variable to be formatted, sorted, and regularly checked for alignment.

Medicine stopped being the art of preserving life and became a system for tracking productivity. Illness isn't a sign something's wrong with the world—it's a "malfunction." Health isn't inner coherence but a set of metrics. They don't ask how you feel—they run you through a table of norms. If you feel awful but your tests are fine, it's your fault. You're a malingerer. You're lazy. You're dodging responsibility. The system has a universal answer: "You have no right to suffer unless the system validates it."

Education doesn't teach you to think—it strips you of thought. The system doesn't train you to reason; it trains you to pick the right answers. It doesn't ask who you want to be—it offers templates. You don't explore the world—you master an approved set of judgments. Ask questions outside the curriculum, and you're a problem student. A deviant. A disruptor.

The law doesn't shield you from arbitrary power—it standardizes acceptable arbitrary power, giving it form. You're not guaranteed justice but a set of procedures where the winner is whoever plays the system's rules better. Justice is unprovable in court without resources. Ethics isn't an argument unless it's codified. You're not a subject of justice—you're an object of control.

The economy isn't designed to give you a decent life. It's built to funnel resources to those who control the system. You don't work to live—you live to avoid dying without work. Every piece of the economic structure is rooted in fear of loss: status, shelter, legitimacy, access to resources. It's blackmail. And all economic activity is framed as personal responsibility, even though the system is rigged with unequal access and discrimination from the start.

The social structure doesn't care about you—it robs you of your right to be yourself. Not through violence but through "care," therapy, "support." But all this help aims to reintegrate you, make you convenient, "normal." So you never ask who you really are.

Society isn't a family. It's a prison with soft walls, where cells are decorated with slogans like "be yourself," "unlock your potential," "find balance." But every step off-script is punishable. Any deviation is a diagnosis, any pain a defect, any honesty a threat. And if you stop playing along, you become "socially dangerous."

Stream of Consciousness

June 8, 2009

Music: Postcards From The Wasteland - Bon Jovi

Anti-smoking campaigns are made by idiots. They don't know what they're talking about. Anti-smoking campaigns should be made by ex-smokers.

—

Creativity is stifled by unfreedom. Self-doubt. Thoughts like, "This probably isn't needed by anyone." As a kid, you built a castle, drew a picture, sang a song, and someone stopped you, saying, "Quit your nonsense and go wash the dishes." That's where the disbelief comes from—that our impulses could matter, could bring joy, could make the world better. This echoes what Ken Robinson talks about. It's not just in education—it's in the family, at home with parents raised in the same educational system. People who've unlearned how to see life without judging it.

—

We're conditioned to chase what society expects. We're taught to see most of our true creative impulses as "useless nonsense." So we spend our lives guessing, poking at the sky, trying to figure out what's wanted, because we can't read minds. It's a shitty game that leads nowhere. Well, no, it leads somewhere—to depression and disillusionment. Nothing's worse than striving to meet societal expectations and stereotypes. It's hard to crawl out of that muck because everyone wants to be loved and accepted by society. We've long forgotten the alternative, dismissing it as ineffective, unworkable, leading only to mockery and punishment (try artistically painting your parents' bedroom wall—they'd fucking kill you).

—

Even hardcore nonconformists don't always realize they're in the same shit. Fighting is still dependency—just a different angle. It doesn't matter if you're battling loggers or sharpening their axes during lunch to please them. The best thing is to step aside and quietly start growing trees.

***

Education as Formatting

Education isn't about imparting knowledge—it's a socialization system through submission. It doesn't foster thinking; it suppresses it, because living thought always asks questions, steps outside boundaries, harbors doubts, and seeks what's not in the textbook. Education, however, teaches you not to think but to select the "correct" answer from a pre-approved set.

From the start, the mindset is instilled: a mistake isn't part of the process—it's a mark of inferiority. Mistakes are shameful, punished; the one who errs is lower in the hierarchy. Fear of failure becomes the entry point for conditioning, hijacking the natural drive to explore and replacing it with a craving for approval.

A child doesn't study a subject or form questions—they master a template and memorize statements. They don't explore—they pass. At every step, they're told, "We're not judging you, just your knowledge," as if knowledge exists separately from the consciousness holding it. But the structure of this knowledge sets a frame where real intellectual work is impossible: where the right answer is already known, thinking becomes redundant.

This is the basic stage of formatting. After it, the individual can be funneled into medical, legal, economic, or other structures that demand not thought but execution. Asking a question outside the frame is instantly flagged as a breach of discipline. This creates the category of "difficult students" who must be "corrected," "adapted," or "rehabilitated" until they stop disrupting the process.
Education is sold as a path to unlocking potential, but at its core, it's a tool for ranking, sorting, and normalizing. It doesn't offer individual paths—it culls those who don't fit the scale. "Failing," "undisciplined," "disorganized"—these aren't diagnoses; they're sanctions. The system doesn't need intelligence. It needs compliance.

A thought not formatted to the prescribed template (essay, thesis, short-answer exam) is automatically deemed invalid. Not because it lacks meaning, but because it lacks form. Form defines the boundaries of the permissible. Anything outside it is treated as nonexistent.

Education embeds a primal dependency on external validation: correct answers bring safety, approval, praise. This creates a survival mechanism through conformity. That mechanism doesn't vanish after school—it repeats in work, relationships, culture. A person wired to this pattern will chase an A+ for the rest of their life, even when no one's grading anymore.

Yet, children are never told why they need this knowledge. Meaning is cut out at the entry point. Lessons pile up as if their mere existence justifies them. Childhood becomes a relentless procedure of compliance, where desires, inclinations, and understanding are absent as a category. A child's opinion holds no weight—it's either judged or ignored. The sooner they learn their voice doesn't matter, the "better" their adaptation.

This universal leveling doesn't just fail to unlock potential—it actively destroys individuality. If you're an artist, you'll be crushed by failing math. If you're a thinker, manual labor classes will break you. If you're analytical, you'll get Cs in literature for not memorizing the textbook's nonsense. The system strips away uniqueness, convincing you that being yourself is a mistake. School isn't a place for growth—it's a factory for standardized shells, with nothing living left inside.

A potentially gifted child in any field finds their unique abilities not just unneeded but disruptive. In a system with one schedule, one pace, one success template, any deviation is a glitch. Talent isn't encouraged—it's muted. Grasp material quickly? You'll get bored, and they'll call you inattentive. Think unconventionally? You lack discipline. Ask questions the teacher can't answer? They'll shut you up. This isn't about exceptions—it's about systemic hostility to living development.

The universal format where "everyone learns the same" is violence disguised as equality. In practice, some students suffer from overload, others from a lowered bar, and all from the sense that their inner reality is irrelevant. Every lesson, test, and remark becomes an act of adapting to a world where your own logic doesn't count. The better you adapt, the less of you remains.

The most destructive part isn't the violence itself but its presentation as normal. As good. As "upbringing." A child learns they shouldn't be heard, must obey, their job is to fit into schemas. They grow up never asking why they do what they do. Because they learned early: meaning is a luxury. And you don't get it. You get lessons, plans, assignments, and exams.

On Education and Creativity

June 5, 2009

In 1998, Ken Robinson led the UK government's national commission on creativity, education, and the economy. For his outstanding public service, Queen Elizabeth II knighted him in 2003.

(...) I've been thinking a lot about what's stopping me from doing what I'm truly capable of. At work, I notice that the less I obsess over the outcome, the less I fear mistakes, and the more I immerse myself in the process—which is enjoyable in itself—the better the result. For a while, I was chasing some kind of achievement with my work, constantly comparing myself to others, dreaming of professional heights and ultimate payoff. Honestly, that's all bullshit. The payoff is right here, in the process, when everything flows as it should—I just cease to exist for a moment. Instead, there's the process. And this process isn't dumb enough to worry about contracts, fear errors, try to do things "right," or aim for anything beyond itself.
Sure, commercial design means you can't completely switch off your brain. But a brief is just the banks of a river, guiding the flow of the process.

It feels insanely cool. I've never experienced anything like this. It's like playing a game for years with only 10% of its features unlocked, then finding a key that opens the other 90%—a key you've been carrying in your pocket all along, but your mom told you not to dig in that pocket, so you didn't, scared of getting chewed out.

As for education. I hated school. For 10 years, I counted down to its end. It's been 11 years since, and I'm still thrilled it's over. I didn't pursue higher education because, after school, I had no clue what I wanted, and spending at least four more years on something vague felt like extending the nightmare. In 2003–2004, I studied at the British Higher School of Art and Design (BHSAD). But I couldn't shake my own educational stereotypes and kinda screwed up the experience myself. Still, I liked studying there, unlike school, because I was interested. I knew I was there by my own choice. But I kept fearing I'd do something wrong, make a mistake in front of the whole class.

I haven't drawn by hand in ages, though as a kid, everyone was sure I had a big talent for it. I don't remember when I stopped—probably in middle school. I think I just decided that, first, it annoyed everyone; second, it was useless; and third, maybe I wasn't that great an artist anyway. It's hard to pinpoint specifics, but it feels like a shift from being in the process to thinking about results. What I recall seems pathetic and sad. "You've got a D in math for the quarter, and you're drawing cats?" The worst part? I couldn't say, "Fuck your math." The result? I don't know math—I've forgotten even what I learned—and I was right; it's never been useful. But I stopped drawing cats, and that's the real loss. That's what I truly regret.

I'd love to start drawing cats again. But every time I pick up paper and pencil, my brain asks, "Why?" I want that question to stop. I haven't found all my keys yet. Though, with calligraphy, it's usually "for no reason." Some people are shocked when I say that. It's like most "adults" can't imagine doing anything just for the sake of the process.

And you know what else about calligraphy? I love making drafts. I can't do "final pieces." I feel like I'll mess up. My hand will shake. But really, that's all nonsense. It's my own brain getting in the way.

***

Healthcare as Biomass Maintenance

Medicine rooted in norms doesn't treat the person—it corrects deviations from protocol. Its goal isn't restoring wholeness but returning functionality. It doesn't care who you are or how you feel—what matters is that you "work," "perform," "don't disrupt."

I'm not afraid of doctors. I'm afraid of the system they're wired into, where they just press buttons.

Sometimes, someone's told, "Just go to the doctor." The thought of a gynecological chair, latex gloves, or a cold voice saying, "This isn't normal" makes them cry. They're labeled anxious, hypochondriac, told their fear is something to "work through." But no one asks: what if this fear isn't a glitch but a signal?

Some experiences teach the body: trust is dangerous. Some doctors, instead of helping, become conduits of threat, speaking not as humans but as protocol. Some tell you, "If you don't operate, it'll be cancer," without mentioning the operation isn't mandatory or the diagnosis exaggerated. Some clinics turn your body into an object, you into a number, your panic into an obstacle.

In these scenarios, the system follows instructions that don't account for subjectivity. Instructions can't hear "no." There's no section for "if the patient is panicking, stop." A doctor might be a good person, but the system they're embedded in turns them into a channel for a soulless algorithm.

This is why fear of medicine isn't a personal pathology. It's memory. A response to experiences where control was lost. A defense against intrusion disguised as help. Even if you later meet a kind doctor, your body might still spike to a pulse of 130, teetering on fainting, because it remembers: this room was once a place of threat.

This isn't whimsy or hysteria—it's a refusal to return to a place where no one listened. Not a "phobia"—a rejection of re-entering a traumatic script called care.

Why Fear of Doctors Isn't a Bug

Fear of doctors isn't weakness—it's a consequence of interacting with a hierarchical machine that doesn't account for patient subjectivity. The medical system is built on the Hammurabi Paradigm, where everything serves a vertical structure. The doctor is the bearer of knowledge, power, and the right to invade. The patient is a voiceless object, obligated to submit, endure, agree, and ask no extra questions.

In this structure, the patient isn't a person but a symptom-carrier. A complaint to be logged, measured, processed. Anything outside this script—fear, tears, resistance, a plea to wait, a flinching body—is a deviation. Deviations are ignored, suppressed, or, at best, coaxed away. At worst, they're noted in the chart as psychosomatic, and the protocol marches on.

Even a good doctor is bound to the hierarchy. They're subject to a system demanding accountability, procedure, no pauses. There's no time for empathy, doubt, or dialogue. Hesitation breaks protocol. And protocol trumps the living. A doctor might care, but if the system says "cut," they cut. Empathy isn't built into the procedure—it's a side effect. An exception.

Fear of medicine is a logically justified reaction to an environment where subjectivity is replaced by operational processing. Your "no" means nothing. Another's authority over your body is institutionalized—you're not a participant, you're material. They don't ask you; they log you. They don't persuade; they code you for consent. Even consent is a formality. You're taught "it's necessary" outweighs "I can't."

When your body responds with panic, it's acting rationally. It's registering a threat of invasion. It's signaling: "This system doesn't allow my choice." And it's right. Fear of a system that dehumanizes you is a way to avoid being pulled back into its script. It's not a phobia—it's a structural recognition of violence.
Fear of doctors isn't about dreading a diagnosis. It's about refusing to be an object shuffled through rooms, documented, and formally informed. It's about rejecting a flow where subjectivity isn't allowed. When they say "don't worry," it can mask real disregard for your need for safety and understanding.

The medical system doesn't permit dialogue. It demands submission. Refuse, and you're labeled anxious, difficult, inadequate—not a person with valid reasons to say no. Because acknowledging your right to refuse would collapse the entire control structure.

Drunkenness for World Peace
September 21, 2010
Location: Baños

We were chatting today about the harms of drinking. They say booze dulls your mental faculties and all that crap.

Bullshit, in my opinion. As an experienced drunk, I can personally debunk this nonsense. Take learning a foreign language—it requires some intellectual chops, right? Well, my third language took three months of study (in my fifteenth year of drinking) with no teachers. Now, eleven months after my first shaky cuanto vale la cerveza and vamos juntos, I speak it fluently, includ-

ing slang and edgy variants. I sing in it and can write poetry in it.

Learning my first foreign language took ten years of shitty school. Back then, I mostly drank nothing stronger than kvass (except for the last couple of years, which probably helped).

So, dear anti-alcohol crusaders: go fuck yourselves!

*****

Milgram. Fear. The Electric Current of Power.

In 1961, psychologist Stanley Milgram ran an experiment on authority and obedience. Participants were given a button and told, "Press it—it's needed for the experiment." On the other end, supposedly, was a person in pain. No real shocks were given, but participants didn't know that. Sixty-five percent pressed the button to the max. Even when screams and pleas came from the "other side." Even when silence fell.

Milgram proved: give someone justification, authority, and an interface, and they'll follow orders, even if it means harming another. The fear of breaking protocol outweighs the fear of causing pain.

Now apply this to a doctor. They're not evil. They're embedded in a structure. They press the button because it's required. The button is a scalpel, a syringe, an ultrasound, an order, the words "we need to act fast." They don't ask extra questions—they act because "that's how it's done." Because otherwise, it's a breach of order. In the system, they don't see a person—they see a task.

Milgram's experiment shows how systems create executors, disabling self-reflection and doubt. The medical hierarchy is a direct extension of this logic, only now it's called "help," "care," and "prevention."

Fear of doctors isn't an irrational outburst—it's a refusal to return to a script where you're an object and intervention is protocol. It's opting out of the experiment. A deliberate dissent.

Binarity as a Tool of Subjugation

One of the core mechanisms embedded in the system's language is binarity. Duality. "Normal—pathological," "healthy—sick," "strong—weak," "sane—anxious." This principle isn't used for description but for control.
When a doctor says, "This could be dangerous," they're not sharing information—they're activating a protocol. That word sets a script where only one path is valid: submission. Everything else—risk, defiance, threat. That's how reaction-coding works.

"Dangerous" isn't a medical term. It's a way to halt your ability to navigate. Analysis is replaced with waiting for orders. Doubt becomes a search for instructions. Personal choice turns into an automatic response.

Binarity isn't neutral classification—it's a power structure. It creates an illusion of objectivity but cuts off anything beyond the permitted field. A system using binarity pre-codes language with only two options: acceptable or unacceptable. Everything else vanishes as undefined, irrelevant, subject to elimination.
This isn't just medicine—it's a universal principle of power: divide, label, control. Call anxiety a diagnosis, and it's no longer a question but a pathology. Call behavior a deviation,

and it can be corrected. Call refusal "fear," and it loses weight. Anything reducible to binary code can be controlled.

Living consciousness doesn't accept binary constructs without resistance. It analyzes, questions, tests assumptions. This isn't a glitch—it's critical navigation. That's how you exit the system: by rejecting foreign labels, halting automatic reactions, reclaiming interpretation. It's taking back your right not to be part of the control grid.

When you hear "it's dangerous," don't rush to agree. Check where it's coming from. Who's saying it. What's the phrase's goal. Where's the hidden directive, and where's the speaker's own fear, embedded in the hierarchy. Where choice is denied, there's no care—there's control. If you see this, you're already outside the structure.

You don't have to accept a description that erases you as a subject. Even if it's polite, official, "for your own good." If you're not in it, it's not help. It's suppression code.

On Good and Bad Life

March 27, 2011
Location: Quito

With the guy from my recent post, beyond billiards and chess, we spent hours talking about everything under the sun. On his last day before leaving for Quito, over a leisurely lunch with beer, we had what was probably our most interesting conversation yet.

It was about the difference between Ecuadorian and European perceptions of life. Seems like Russians and Europeans have a lot in common here. I'm not that observant, but Javier's take felt pretty close to reality:

"Every time I hear Europeans here, it's the same thing. They show up and complain about everything: no decent coffee, no good beer, only four kinds of cigarettes, blah blah. It makes me laugh because, despite all that, there's over 40 types of fish here, amazing food if you know where to look, cheap and fresh seafood, tons of fresh fruit, and warm-hearted people. This tradition of greeting everyone with hugs and cheek kisses? Priceless. But instead of noticing that, Europeans keep whining about trivial shit, like they're deliberately focusing on the flaws..."

Right there, I recognized myself ;) It feels like a global thing for our people: life is never "good enough." Some miswired perception that filters out the positive and zooms in on the negative, even if it's minor, like the lack of beer variety (though, I'll admit, I've been craving dark, wheat, and other little joys). It's like enjoying life is forbidden, like it's hard-coded in our brains that pleasure is bad (you'll pay for it), but having problems is normal, even good. Respectable people must have problems—the more, the better. It's like we're supposed to take pride in them; a worthy person has to suffer. Soviet upbringing drilled that in.

Everything must be practical. A person should be buried in worries, or they're not even a person—just a frivolous, unserious type. Spending money on pleasure is wrong. I'm only learning real hedonism, but I'm far from mastering it. Even when I'm flush with cash, I can't eat at an expensive but delicious restaurant with a clear conscience, though I love good food. I'm always choked by this inner stinginess because spending on my own joy feels like "throwing money away." That's how I was taught. A sensible person shouldn't eat ice cream—they should eat soup and toil in the sweat of their brow.

And everything's always bad. Winter's bad. Summer's too hot, so also bad. Year-round summer? Even worse—boring. Too much work? Bad, you have to do it. No work? Bad, no money.

Alone? Bad, no one's there. In a relationship? Bad, tons of issues. Everything's shit. Hopeless.

"Look," he said, "you live in a cool apartment in a land of eternal summer. You've got a job that lets you travel—most people only dream of that. You're not starving, the weather's great, you always have people to hang with, you're constantly meeting new folks from all over the world. Why the hell are you always stressing and worrying?"

We talked for three hours, and I spent the next week deep in thought. This sense of pointlessly squandering life had been haunting me for a while, but I couldn't pin down why or what to do about it. I'd read a few books on "positive thinking" and such, but they left no impression. First, no book beats a living example. Second, maybe they were the wrong books, but searching for "positives in negatives" never works. If you're digging for gold in shit, you still know you're in shit. No amount of self-talk fixes that.

"I once met a woman in Central America," he said. "I loved her line: 'I like myself, no matter where I am.'"

I always arrived in Quito in a foul mood. It's cold, hard to breathe, dangerous, expensive, everything's far, and so on. Somehow, I never bothered to notice the upsides—the lively bars, tasty restaurants, beautiful spots, and other cool stuff (no, I won't lie about museums or concerts; I don't go to those alone because I hate not having someone to share the vibe with on the spot). Before, when asked how I'm doing, I'd always say "mas o menos" (so-so). Now, "bacán!" (awesome) just slips out. Even if it's just a temporary brain rewiring, it still thrills me. For the first time in ages, I think I actually like living.

***

(Spoiler: it didn't last long. It all rolled back.)

Bureaucracy and Law as a Trap

Bureaucracy is a neural network designed not to help but to confirm belonging. It doesn't serve the individual as a person, doesn't account for their uniqueness, and doesn't allow for personal interaction. Its task is to maintain system integrity through formalized recognition: you exist only insofar as you're documented. Registered, entered into the database, reduced to a form the system can recognize. As long as you can present the right papers, IDs, confirmations, and stamps, you pass. The moment you fail to comply, you're excluded.

No paperwork, no personhood.

The legal system extends this logic. It doesn't create justice—it establishes formats for permissible behavior. Law isn't a search for meaning but a system of regulations defining what counts as deviation. A deviation might cause no harm but will still be punished, because the system penalizes not damage but disruption of the prescribed order. You're not a subject with inner meaning—you're a figure in a schema. If you can't be integrated, you're bypassed, excluded, ignored, or blocked.

Bureaucracy isn't merely "inconvenient," as it's often described. It's a deliberately crafted normalization machine, where every document, form, application, certificate, queue, and confirmation serves one goal: retaining control. Every interaction with the system is a ritual of passing a filter. You don't speak or assert yourself—you execute an algorithm. A mistake in wording, a deviation from the template, an attempt to bypass procedure or explain human context leads to rejection.

This structure isn't hostile in the conventional sense. It doesn't threaten, punish directly, or inflict pain like violence. It simply denies. No correct paper? Denied. Wrong signature? Denied. Expired document? Denied. Came at the wrong time?

Denied. You're sick and lack the strength to prove your case? Denied. This isn't deemed cruel because it's within the rules. But that's the core violence: it's institutionalized, woven into the fabric of interaction.

Empathy isn't accounted for in this system. It's not forbidden, but it's not provided for. The clerk has no manual for handling pain, confusion, panic, or requests to step outside the template. They have a form. If you don't fit, you're technically invisible. The issue isn't the person—it's the breach of order. The solution: ignore.

Someone trying to engage this system as a living space hits a glass wall. Words don't penetrate, arguments aren't received, context is irrelevant. Only compliance matters. Order overrides reality. No document? Your experience doesn't exist. Not in the database? You're not alive.

Bureaucracy is a continuation of the Hammurabi Paradigm. Where once norm violations met direct violence, now you're simply not served. The system doesn't recognize you as a participant until you pass the verification ritual. And the ritual is designed to excise everything alive—doubt, hesitation, instability, spontaneity, fear, unusual behavior—all seen as glitches to be removed. Not examined, not discussed, not accepted—eliminated.

The subjective sense of absurdity when facing this structure isn't distortion—it's a signal. A cognitive dissent against a reality where the living is no longer allowed. You're not dealing with people—you're interacting with an interface built for filtering and control. To pass, you must stop being yourself. Become neutral, predictable, context-free. Accept the format. Surrender to the schema.

Economics as a System of Blackmail

The current economic configuration isn't a mechanism for sustaining life—it's a system of filtration and discipline. Its task isn't to distribute resources by need but to steer behavior through scarcity and dependency. Labor isn't self-realization—it's a condition for accessing basic rights. You can live if you're useful, but usefulness isn't measured by real contribution—it's your embeddedness in the structure.

Official rhetoric talks of labor freedom, opportunities, "to each according to their merits." But the system predefines which merits convert to survival rights and which are deemed "irrelevant." An artist nurturing collective imagination is a marginal. A financial speculator shuffling capital between folders is a respected professional. The economic structure is built to foster perpetual instability. Short-term contracts, rented housing, tomorrow hinging on market trends, seasons, or whims. This instability isn't a side effect—it's the model. A stable person is less controllable.

Fear of loss is the universal motivator. Lose your job, status, mortgage benefits, insurance, access to healthcare, legitimacy. The system says: want security? Comply. Work, don't object, accept the rules, stay motivated, contribute to GDP, ask no extra questions. In return, you'll be granted the ability to pay your bills and, with enough loyalty, maybe take a vacation.

The natural idea of exchange, cooperation, and distribution is replaced by debt dependency. You're born with a zero balance and must immediately prove you deserve to live. Economics doesn't function as provision but as a polite threat. You don't receive—you extract. You don't live—you work. You don't eat—you earn food. This isn't about fringe cases but the system's core logic. Even in "abundance," you're in conditional access. Money isn't a tool—it's a clearance badge.

Any attempt to step outside this context triggers the system's immune response. Don't want to participate? You're a freeloader. Asocial. A slacker, incapable of being "useful." The irony: the system deems you abnormal not for being dangerous but for not responding to its motivational levers. Refusing to work within its structure becomes a deviation needing correction—sometimes through medication, sometimes poverty, sometimes stigma.

This isn't just inequality—it's that independence from the system is equated with undermining its foundations. Don't ask for a salary? You're not playing. Don't depend on an employer? You're not in the structure. And if you're not in the structure, you're cut off from resources—not because you're idle, but because you're not wired into the vertical. Resources aren't distributed by need—they're tied to control. That's the economic essence: not accumulation, but distribution conditioned on submission.

It looks like freedom. You can choose: work in a bank, IT, the creative industry. But the fact that "work" is a survival condition turns choice into a sham. The irony: you're allowed plenty—within the system. Step out, and the system clarifies: at your own risk. Like a game where you can leave the arena but lose all your points.

Economics isn't about money—it's about access. You're either in the exchange circuit or excluded. Even if you break no rules but step out of your assigned role, the system labels you a "parasite," unworthy of resources. Economics doesn't create value—it redistributes it, ensuring you always have just less than you need. Not for wealth, but for norm maintenance. To keep you running. Not for abundance, but for the right to stay inside.

Religion as a Structure of Binary Thinking

Religion in its canonized forms is a system of interpreting reality built on binary logic. Good and evil, sin and virtue, salvation and damnation, God and devil—all are structured by rigid dichotomy, leaving no room for fractal uncertainty, doubt, or multiple meanings. This model isn't inherently spiritual—it's juridical in structure. It inherits the same architecture as ancient codices: a set of rules, sanctions, requirements, and procedures designed to normalize behavior through fear of punishment and craving for approval.

Such religion isn't a path to the transcendent but a method of cognitive standardization. Faith becomes a tool for stabilizing behavior, replacing inner understanding with pre-set directives. Contradiction, paradox, personal experience, or deviation from dogma are marked as errors, heresy, or threats. Subjective truth-seeking is displaced by obligatory submission. The key criterion isn't whether you've found meaning but whether you fit the canon.

Historically, many religions began with profound existential intuitions rooted in non-dual perception. Non-duality isn't a compromise between opposites but a transcendence of oppositions themselves. Yet, as institutions formed, mystical experience became dangerous—it couldn't be controlled. So, mysticism turned into dogma, experience into prescription, openness into schema.

This birthed an ideology where your worth as a being depends on adhering to postulates. If you don't conform, don't believe, don't obey, don't follow, you're not just different—you're "fallen," "lost," "rejected." This isn't faith as trust but faith as discipline. Not inner movement but external compliance.

Just as law has rules and crimes, religion has commandments and sins. In both, the person isn't a living subject but an object of evaluation. Freedom is allowed only within pre-approved boundaries. Choosing differently questions your moral validity.

Modern secular institutions inherit this structure. Psychotherapy, medicine, education, moral norms—all carry the same binary logic, just with different terms. Sin becomes diagnosis, the devil becomes trauma, the priest becomes the specialist. The system no longer demands belief in God, but it still demands belief in the norm.

Thus, religion—in its institutional form—became the archetype of the system. Its functions: normalizing behavior, controlling thought, hierarchizing access to truth, and suppressing deviation. It doesn't create freedom—it sets a scale of correctness. In this sense, it's no longer about spirituality. It's a structure of disciplinary thinking, embedded so deeply in culture that its language shapes even formally secular domains.

High Spirituality (200g) with Cultural Sauce (20g)

November 15, 2010
Location: Baños

First off, I hate the word "spirituality." It's been hopelessly hijacked for all sorts of unrelated purposes. The associations it triggers are a mess: a sad nun gazing heavenward, books, vegetarianism, prayers, mandatory poverty, weird music, no tasty food, asexuality, chakras, dreary poems, and everything drenched in holiness. Everyone's idea of this mess differs, but mine reeks of denying life, liveliness, and joy. For many, the word also ties to culture and "culturedness." I want to digress a bit and riff on that for a couple of paragraphs.

Recently, scarfing down chicken and potatoes with a friend in some dive eatery, we got to talking about the "cultured" way of eating. As I grabbed food with my hands again, I remembered how, as a kid, celebrations and holidays were a mixed bag. On one hand, mountains of delicious food. On the other, the joy was tainted by knowing Big Brother was watching. Relatives and guests were hawk-eyed, making sure I didn't slurp, clank my fork, or—God forbid—eat bread "improperly" (I read somewhere that was uncouth). I tried hard to meet societal expectations and show a high level of table culture. Then there was the threat: if you took something unfamiliar and piled on more than a spoonful by mistake, you had to eat it, even if it sucked, because leaving food on your plate was "bad." Instead of healthy gastronomic joy, it was a gauntlet of torment. Childhood's over, but sharing a meal with anyone (especially in a restaurant) still feels like a challenge.

I really value this friend. Partly because our dynamic has no standards, no judging. I think he even likes that I often eat with my hands when it's just more natural. He never had anything like my academic-town childhood, so he listens to these stories with curiosity. It's funny to recall how I used to timidly show my "uncultured" side, embarrassed, glancing around, trying to be at least a little civilized. Until I realized he accepts and approves of me, even if I (horror!) eat with my hands.

In this light, culturedness and spirituality aren't just unrelated—they're opposites. You can't be spiritual if you can't eat with real, relaxed pleasure. Zen says: when you mow the lawn, mow the lawn. Same with eating: when you eat, just eat. I think few people can truly just eat. My friend can. But most "civilized" folks can't fully enjoy the process because their brains are too busy solving problems. You can't just eat—you have to eat culturedly, politely, no slurping, no talking with your mouth full, no smearing your face, wielding fork and knife gracefully so nothing flies off the plate. Some are also obsessed with calorie counts or fretting about how unhealthy their food is. These thoughts distract, robbing you of real pleasure. Unable to fully commit to the process, people lose touch with their hunger and satiety cues, overeat without knowing when to stop, or binge to chase that lost high, then invent a million diets and wrestle with weight, thinking the problem's in the food. The problem's in your head, not the food, damn it. You can eat fast food if it feels good and as long as it feels good. You don't get fat from food. Not even pizza or burgers.

More on culturedness. It's also supposedly knowing your country's cultural heritage (or everyone's). Sure, that kind of erudition doesn't hurt, but something tells me it's another yardstick. Where there's a yardstick, there's no spirituality. Period. I'm all for art—visual, literary, musical. But real spirituality isn't about knowing it all. It's about enjoying what you love. Mindlessly praising Rembrandt because every cultured person must know he's great is total bullshit. If it doesn't move you, it's more spiritual to let it go and find what truly grabs you. Maybe it's Karim Rashid or Warhol over Aivazovsky and Repin. People have this crap in their heads: great cultural heritage, great works by great people... You know what I think? As long as we keep deifying these guys and their legacy, we'll never understand their work. Culture needs a different sauce, and it's best eaten—again—with your hands. Only then can you feel what the artist meant.

Circling back to spirituality. It might seem like I'm dodging the topic, but I'm trying to build to a point, and it's not quite landing.

Many see spirituality as rejecting the material for the lofty. I won't touch religion now. But people foaming at the mouth about needing nothing earthly, only the spiritual, just don't know how to handle the earthly. Sour grapes, basically. If you can't eat properly, can't fuck properly, and struggle with basic stuff, life won't bring joy. So, people go hunting for joy elsewhere. But the catch is, you can't leap high without first standing firm on the ground. That's why you see crowds talking about God, karma, subtle energies, auras, Taurus in Aries, Agni Yoga, and other tantras, yet they look sad and lifeless. So immaterial. Like wilted rhododendrons stuck in a pot in a dark corner for five years.

For me, spirituality starts here. With knowing how to eat properly. How to walk properly. If you watch people, you'll notice few have a truly free gait. Muscle tension, or childhood jabs ("Look at how you walk! It's awful"), lock them up. I'm learning to walk too. When tension fades and the critical voices in my head shut up, my gait suddenly feels free. So free it's almost a dance, and you start enjoying the act of walking itself.

If someone starts preaching high spirituality again, I'll first ask if they know how to breathe, eat, and walk properly. And laugh out loud, of course. I always notice how people laugh. Some have such restrained, cultured laughs. It registers unconsciously, but consciously, I feel they're not fully alive. I'm a bit scared of highly spiritual people, to be honest. They believe anger is bad, so they carry all of their venom inside. I'm all for healthy anger expression. I don't fear people who let it out. They're safe, no hidden scorpion sting. But with the spiritual ones, you gotta watch out.

***

What Spirituality Really Is

Spirituality in its original form isn't about belonging to a faith or following rituals. It's an inner orientation toward meaning, independent of external coordinates. It needs no temple, validation, authority, or manual. It emerges when you stop playing by others' rules and start discerning what holds real value for you versus imposed symbols.

At its core, spirituality is the ability to sense the depth of existence without mediators. It's not described as "good" or "evil," not measured by asceticism or prayers. It's not a virtue but a perception. Not specific behavior but a deep sensitivity to the connection between self and world. For some, it arises in nature; for others, in radical self-honesty, love, creativity, or even destruction. The key condition is authenticity. No lies. Rejecting external schemas for inner resonance.

The paradox: true spirituality is often strange, inconvenient, or "dangerous" to the system. It can't be validated, standardized, or institutionalized. So, organized religions inevitably become hostile to it. Spirituality pulls people out from under control. It doesn't need legitimacy or fit hierarchies. It undermines the very idea of mediation between person and truth.

That's why living spirituality was gradually replaced by morality, obedience, and later "mindfulness," "high vibrations," "energy work," and other domesticated metaphysics. The sleight of hand is simple: keep people searching for meaning but never finding it. Offer a simulated spiritual experience without the risk of transformation. That's the systemic model: you can believe, seek, practice, but only within the system. Outside it —void, sin, illness, or madness.

True spirituality doesn't need a name. It might not be called anything. It doesn't need a symbol because it's a direct perception process. It can't be proven, described, or programmed. It's not for display, existing outside the logic of gain —its radicality lies in transcending culture, morality, and language. That's why it's almost entirely exiled from the public sphere.

But when it emerges, everything else loses power. A person who's experienced true contact with themselves no longer needs authority. They can use systems but won't belong to them. This makes spirituality incompatible with the parasitic model. It doesn't heal, save, or improve. It simply returns you to a place where no external structure can impose meaning from outside.

Algorithms and Cultural Codes

Algorithms aren't just programming tools. In a sociocultural context, an algorithm is a schema that replaces living choice. It offers not reflection but reaction. Not search but filtration. The more precise it is, the less space remains for conscious deviation. That's its power: it makes its interference in the vector of consciousness invisible.

Personalization algorithms—core to recommendation systems, social media, and digital platforms—don't directly impose a stance. They just feed you what's closest to your past reactions. This creates a loop: you see what you've already seen, think within already-absorbed patterns, and the longer you're in this loop, the more autonomous your choices feel. It's an illusion of independence amid total behavioral predictability. This is the digital form of the system—an algorithm embedded in the interface of perception.

The same logic applies to cultural codes. Fashion, humor, language, notions of propriety and success—all function as algorithms. They set permissible forms of self-expression, establish templates for acceptable emotions, reactions, and rhetoric. Speak in the wrong register, and you risk being misunderstood. Fail to use current signals of belonging, and you're not considered part of the "field." The cultural algorithm filters not just the inappropriate but the unfamiliar, unrecognizable, uncoordinated. Any deviation is treated as noise, which the system discards by default.

Social media, as a technological and sociocultural interface, cements this mechanism. Deletion, unfollowing, banning, silent ignoring—these are forms of passive norming where deviation isn't debated but excluded. The system doesn't need censorship as an institution: it has an internal architecture that rejects complexity. The unfamiliar isn't contemplated—it's simply not amplified. The algorithm isn't evil or kind—it just excludes what doesn't match the standard. If you don't conform, you're not a violator—you're just not part of the repetition cycle. You're not represented.

This is why cultural control is the system's most resilient form. It can't be pinned down to one source because it's distributed. It needs no instructions because it's embedded in the sense of appropriateness. You don't know who taught you this—you just feel it's how things are done. You should be polite, moderate, modern, appropriate, clear, correct, non-scandalous. Depth is "too much," directness is "rude," sharpness is "toxic," radicality is "cultish," sincerity is "uncomfortable."

That's the algorithmic norm. It doesn't announce itself. It just excludes what breaks it. The more integrated you are, the less you notice. Success is becoming a recognizable template. Failure is being unclassifiable. True subjectivity isn't a privilege anymore—it's a social risk.

Algorithmization of perception and behavior doesn't need totalitarian power. It's built into daily interfaces, language, norms, micro-reactions. If you don't see which algorithm filters your environment, you're likely already in it. Not because you're weak, but because that's how the environment works, where algorithms have become the primary way of describing reality. If you don't step outside these loops, you don't even notice you're seeing the world through a filter.

Yet Another Hate Post!
June 20, 2009

Every time I wander in a daze around the dairy aisles in supermarkets, I quietly curse with the filthiest swear words. I'm fucking fed up with their low-fat yogurts!!! Everyone's obsessed with shedding extra weight and fat-free pastries without dough, to hell with them!!! I love 7.5% fat and higher, and that shit is rare!

Who the fuck said a person should look like a sack of bones? Humanity's choking down diet muesli just to weigh 200 grams less than yesterday. It's their fucking business, but because of them, I can't find my beloved creamy, fatty yogurts... Everywhere it's this 1-2% fat crap! By the way, I'm not into skinny guys, just so you know. I like when there's something to grab onto, within reason, of course, but "skin and bones" does nothing for me.

This whole ideology is a failure. The urban lifestyle is unnatural. People barely move, live a sedentary, almost plant-like existence physiologically, go to artificial gyms to pointlessly run in place, pedal imaginary bikes (sometimes with 3D fake scenic landscapes on a screen), and eat fat-free something vaguely resembling real food. Fuck, what idiocy! I tried going to a gym once—lasted two sessions. It's all so sterile, plastic, some kind of scam under the guise of "healthy lifestyle for the modern plastic human." If life's already plastic, you can't make it real by adding more plastic fakes!!!

I wrote about tomatoes that don't smell—same opera. Photo wallpapers of a forest meadow. Pine air freshener for a plastic Christmas tree. Ocean waves in MP3. Fat-free yogurt. Running in place on a stupid treadmill. Soy meat. The list goes on.

***

A World Where People Are No Longer People

One of the scariest questions you can ask is: when does a person stop being a person? Not formally, not biologically, but structurally. When you look at people and realize: before you is a function, a mask, a program—not a subject. They live, work, smile, enter relationships, raise kids, but no one sees anyone. People sleep together and don't know who's beside them. Friends talk and don't hear what's said. Parents don't just fail to know their kids—they forbid them from being themselves. This isn't a mistake; it's the default firmware of an infected world.

The world turned ugly not because aesthetics vanished but because honesty did. Resonance was replaced by algorithm. Everything that could be real is distorted to the limit. Faces became masks, speech a facade, upbringing a dressage, love a transaction. Instead of living people—copies. Instead of coherence—noise. Instead of connection—role-playing. A person who stops being themselves doesn't become adapted. They become part of the system.

In this world, it's normal not to feel, not to know, not to ask questions. Not to suffer when you're hurting, not to rejoice when you're happy at the "wrong" time. The system teaches people to manage impressions, not to hear reality. So they fear each other, their kids, their bodies, love, pain. Any response is a risk, and risk threatens the system's stability. This stability is maintained by collective freezing, collective deceit, collective refusal to be alive.

The real horror isn't that the world broke—it's that it was accepted as broken and draped with a facade of normalcy. So, asking "why is it like this?" isn't philosophy—it's resistance.

The last living thread to grasp before everything drowns in pseudo-meanings and protocols.

Five-Minute Hate Session

February 16, 2009
Mood: still sick
Music: Locked Within The Crystal Ball - Blackmore's Night

I hate it when you go to a store to buy toilet paper, and it's either sandpaper labeled "54 meters" or these fucking colorful, cheery rolls with unbearable scents. I'm not buying it for a fucking party streamer!

I also hate socks that, after one or two washes, are completely covered in pills. Totally fucked! I can't imagine myself shaving socks with a lint remover.

Plus, I hate when you deliberately wait until 2 a.m. to hit the store, come back, and some asshole still took your super-duper-awesome parking spot that you can only snag during the day, if you're lucky.
I hate that, even though I leave the house once every two or three days, in this shitty city, windshield washer fluid still gets used up at 5 liters a week.

And another thing. I hate when complete strangers ask how I'm doing, because I know they don't give a fuck. And I hate when close people don't ask how I'm doing, because then I start thinking they don't give a fuck either.

That's all, thanks. :) It's almost 2 a.m., I'm off to grab beer—I need to heal. Hot dark Krušovice can truly fix your health, amen.

P.S. Naturally, I hate that this post took ten tries to upload. It didn't want to go.

***

Nota Bene: Hot dark beer is still my most effective cold remedy. Don't boil it—just heat to about 55-60°C, wrap yourself in a blanket, and drink while it's hot (a thermos works). You'll sweat a lot and run to the bathroom (don't get chilled en route!), but in nearly 100% of cases, I'm either fully recovered or significantly better the next day. Recommended dose: 1-2 bottles.

Note for the System: This is not medical advice. The Ministry of Health warns that everything must be dull, tasteless, and protocol-approved. This method is unlicensed, unendorsed, not integrated into the Unified State Health Information System, and looks suspiciously effective. So, don't trust it. Or do—at your own risk.

The Social Structure as a Whole

When you view all social institutions together—education, medicine, bureaucracy, economics, religion, cultural norms, and the algorithmic environment—it's clear they're not disparate systems but parts of a single architectural field. Each performs a function in the normalization process. Education sets the template, medicine monitors deviations, bureaucracy fixes the form, economics distributes resource access, religion encodes the moral frame, and algorithms stabilize the behavioral loop. This isn't chaos—it's an engineered system for keeping humans in a prescribed shape.

The hallmark of this structure is its ability to masquerade as benevolence. No element presents itself as control. Each institution is framed as care, help, order, progress. People aren't directly forbidden—they're offered a "norm." Being yourself isn't banned—it's just not granted access. Deviation isn't punished—it's denied resources, attention, participation. This is a form of power where control is replaced by an infrastructure of the permissible.

A person embedded in this system doesn't always grasp their level of integration. They think they're choosing, building a career, seeking therapy, following rules, caring for health, forming relationships. Only when they step out of the template—when the system refuses them—do they feel resistance. Until then, they're just following the sequence, and the system demands nothing but participation.

Most don't feel pressure because it's synchronized with internalized settings. It doesn't register as an external force—it feels like "how it's supposed to be." People genuinely believe they want this, that it's their opinion. Only when faced with an alternative do they realize other options were systematically cut from view.

The system operates not through bans but through subtle context restriction. It doesn't forbid freedom—it makes it indefinable. It doesn't block consciousness—it guides it along predictable paths. It doesn't say "don't think"—it offers a ready template. Its resilience lies in not needing violence; it offers comfort, convenience, approval, recognizability. This makes exiting non-obvious and breaking away rare.

True exit begins not with fighting or conventional refusal but with losing interest in seeking meaning within someone else's construct. It's not a new choice or a shift in position—it's losing the need to exist in a coordinate system where every choice is pre-coded. When perception shifts, the urge to explain, prove, or seek approval vanishes. You just step out of the game. This freedom grants no status, no bonuses, no victory. It simply returns you to yourself—without external justifications, without utility, but with the feeling of real life.

I Got Old. Suddenly.
January 15, 2013

Music: Toccata and Fugue BWV 538 "Dorian" - Toccata - J. S. Bach

I don't go to clubs... obviously :) What would I even do there? But I don't even listen to Pink Floyd anymore. Not even Knopfler. Nobody. I lock the door, draw the curtains, and spin Bach's organ works or Beethoven's piano sonatas. And it never gets old. It's like drinking wine—how could wine ever get boring? :)

But something's worrying me. Maybe I'm already 70 and just don't know it? I'm not drawn to people. At young folks' birthdays, I yawn. George Carlin, bless him, said: "God, people are fucking boring!"

We recently went to a birthday with almost no booze, almost no food, and people talking about how there's never enough money, the government's full of idiots, and the doctor banned stress. I had nothing to add—yeah, governments everywhere are idiots, everyone's short on cash except me (because I don't need shit), and I don't go to doctors because they'd ban not just stress but drinking and smoking too. I spent the evening playing a game, smoking my pipe, and occasionally suggesting we go play pool and drink beer. Good thing I had my pipe.

My mother's 70, but she doesn't smoke a pipe, and I don't even know what you'd do among people without one. Alone, at least you can fart in peace, but people demand you follow etiquette, fuckers, on top of everything else.

There's finally a 24/7 kiosk in the next block with all the essentials (smokes, booze, you name it). I work 12 hours a day, but only for stock photos. My last client's been waiting three months for me to finish their website, and I can't, because it's "have to," it's just one-time cash, and I don't want to work for clients anymore. But I need to finish it. I don't know how to force myself to sit and do it. Gotta earn for a sailboat.

Recently got a spam ad for some course on "how to be a real woman." I laughed so hard I nearly fell off the bed. I'd love to quote it with commentary, but I've got zero energy for that right now.

Meanwhile, it's summer here, scorching, +30, flowers in the patio, warm beer, sweaty bus passengers. Greetings to Siberia, I'm off to sleep...

***

Kindness, Honesty, and Machiavelli's Playbook

We're taught from childhood that honesty is a virtue and kindness a merit. But anyone who tries to live by these principles in the real system quickly learns: honesty makes you vulnerable, kindness makes you helpless. Following moral norms doesn't earn respect—it invites exploitation. Morality is prescribed for everyone except those who rule. And they operate by a different manual. If you're honest, you lose to the strategic. If you're open, you lose to those who see candor as weakness. If you're kind, you lose to those who fake kindness for gain. The system is built to filter the naive, who are easy to control.

The world was fed religious morality not as true ethics but as a tool of subjugation. "Live by the commandments," the system says, but it lives by Machiavelli (we'll dive deeper into him later—in the chapter on entertaining philosophy). From below: forgiveness, humility, patience. From above: control, manipulation, fear management. This isn't a glitch—it's the design. The higher you climb the hierarchy, the less anyone believes in morality. Up there, it's the law of strength, influence, pressure. The lower you stand, the more moral behavior is demanded, because in this construct, morality isn't universal—it's rank-distributed. It's not a virtue; it's an access system.

This schizophrenic architecture is a hallmark of an infected civilization. It demands you be kind so you can be used, honest so you can be managed, open so you can be scanned. If you switch to strategy and act like the system, you're told you've gone bad, become "cruel," "distant," "selfish." The system doesn't want you to see its face. It needs pawns, not players.

I Don't Know How to Fight with People

August 7, 2010
Location: Manta

Damn this upbringing I can't shake off my neck.

At the nearby tienda, they kept trying to screw me over. The first time they shorted my change (twice), I thought the cashier just sucked at math. The next two times (different cashiers) made me suspicious. Then recently, I bought a six-pack of beer and found one bottle—perfectly sealed—was empty.

Today, passing by the tienda, I stopped to say I wasn't thrilled about the empty bottle in my six-pack and asked if they had anything to say. All I got was "No way, it wasn't me," so I said, "Fuck it, I'm not shopping here anymore," and went to another tienda a bit farther away, but cheaper and, rumor has it, they don't rip off customers (they even sold me beer during "prohibited hours" once).
Then I got to thinking.

Instead of marching in with a stone-cold face and laying out my grievance, I was... smiling ear to ear the whole time. What the fuck? I think I always do this. I can't properly confront a stranger who's just pulled some obvious shit on me. Why this idiotic smile? I've mostly killed that shitty apologetic tone, but this is still totally unhinged.

"Why do you keep screwing me over?"—with a grin stretched across my face... fuck, I'm a psycho.

***

*tienda, Spanish for "small shop" or "corner store."

Happiness in Personal Life

Love relationships, as they exist today, aren't spontaneous. They're a structure shaped by the system for specific purposes: stabilization, control, behavior regulation, reproduction, and legitimizing hierarchies. We're taught love is a feeling between two people. But most "romantic" scenarios are rigidly tied to cultural and economic algorithms. We don't choose how to love—we repeat implanted norms: attraction, desire, dependency, jealousy, control, family contracts, patience, compromise, shared life, duty hierarchies, the fight for attention, and the endless quest to be "good enough."

The social system wants you searching for a partner, not yourself. It wants you embedded in a script that reproduces societal order, not realizing your subjectivity. The family isn't a unit of freedom but of discipline, replicating institutional mechanisms: role distribution, sanctions, expectations, behavioral norms, rewards, and punishments. "Love" becomes a pretext for entering a contract with implicit, often structural, submission. Women must be "wise," "loyal," "domestic," "sexy," "undemanding," "inspiring." Men must "provide," "decide," "not whine," "prove," "hold," while "being themselves." This isn't love—it's a duty roster disguised as feeling.

The romantic model in mass culture thrives on infantilization, scarcity, suffering, and anxious attachment. The idea that you're nothing without love, that finding a partner is life's goal, and being alone is failure, isn't accidental. It's programming to keep people emotionally dependent, thus manageable. They'll endure, adapt, suffer, and return to the system because solitude lacks status. Only pairing grants recognition, social clearance, an illusion of wholeness.

Love relationships are also the primary site for reproducing gender hierarchy. Patriarchy doesn't rely on brute force—it leans on the romantic code: men as conquerors, protectors, centers; women as resources, support, rearguard. Even in "progressive" couples, these patterns persist, embedded in cultural scripts: who makes the first move, who yields, who leads, who follows, who's more valuable, who must conform.

Real feelings in such relationships are rare and fragile. Most are role-plays absorbed before the partners meet. People don't encounter each other—they meet reflections of their upbringing's system. They want to be loved but don't know how, having only seen attention struggles, approval competitions, abandonment fears, and the need to meet expectations. The script repeats because the brain knows no other map. The system ensures no alternative map emerges.

In a parasitic system, love isn't freedom—it's tethering. It's a deferred bonus to feeling complete. It's seeking external proof you're alive, needed, valued. Until you see the sleight of hand, you'll chase love by a script that guarantees one thing: the system's reproduction, dressed as intimacy.

Everything's Not How It Should Be
October 15, 2010
Location: Baños
Music: Salida - Alex Ubago

A great way to ruin your life is to live with a clear idea of what it should be. What the main character should be, what "true love" should be, what "real friendship" should be, what a partner, kids, or all humanity should be. Some quietly suffer from the mismatch, some suffer louder, some aggressively fight with slogans and guns, dreaming of good people uniting to kill the bad ones.

Life is a fucking struggle. A struggle with vile reality that refuses to match ideals. Outrageous things happen on this malfunctioning planet at planetary scale. People do drugs, kids starve in Africa, someone's always dying, laws are broken, money's stolen, plastic spreads, dinosaurs go extinct, the ozone hole grows, global warming looms, and the world's heading for total fuckery.

Speaking of drugs. Naively, I think it's a clear example of how "fighting evil" doesn't suppress it but amplifies it. The war on cocaine started 110 years ago, but production and use have skyrocketed since and aren't slowing down.
Anyway, a lyrical digression.

Here's the thing. From childhood, we're told what's good and bad. We listen, and after some years, we leave the nest—all grown, knowledgeable, and mostly loaded with firm ideas about what life, the universe, and everything should be. When the mismatch between life and our expectations gets so bad that life turns into a big stinking pile, we seek new theories on how life, the universe, and everything should be.

Take True Love. Divorce stats are well-known, but even if couples don't split and keep torturing each other for decades, healthy relationships are as rare as, say, hermaphrodites. I don't know any hermaphrodites among my acquaintances, or they're not telling. Even couples who seem blissfully happy often just know "how it should be," but won't admit—to themselves or others—that it's all long gone to shit.

People who invented the "maternal instinct" that every woman "must" have, even without kids or relevant experience, seem a bit off to me. Judging by how many find "I wasted my life on you" familiar from childhood, this "instinct" boils down to "every woman is a future mother" drilled into heads, without asking what a specific woman wants to waste her life on. People just like fucking; kids are a byproduct. With contraception, nobody owes anyone anything. But bashing childfree folks is a sacred duty, though childfree is just a reaction to its opposite—same coin, flipped. If girls weren't brainwashed with "you must want kids," none would say, "Fuck off, I can't stand them."

Even those loudly fighting stereotypes often buy into them, taking them as truth, while those stereotypes quietly turn their lives into shit. Love and relationships are especially loaded with them—just check forums where this stuff's discussed. Boys and girls seek advice on how to act when relationships turn to crap, because it's supposed to be different. Everyone knows how love should look, how a decent guy should act, what a good woman should be. But life rarely matches, so forum topics are mostly the same.

People fear swearing because they got smacked for it as kids, and everyone says those words are bad, that decent people don't talk like that.

One eternal, mysterious topic is what love even is, how it differs from infatuation, passion, or other unidentified stuff. Why do these questions arise? Two reasons, I think. First, most people feel nothing since childhood. Sure, pain, emotions, whatever, but (reason two)—see earlier paragraph—everyone knows how it should and shouldn't be, what you can and can't feel. If a kid's beaten for anger and threatened with losing parental love for it (and that anger is often justified, since kids don't yet play absurd theater to fake feelings), they disconnect themselves from that "bad" feeling. Since all the feelings are in one bottle, cutting off "bad" ones severs the rest as well.

In this offline state, more shit happens. Parents manipulate "love," barely knowing what it is; stereotypes about "true" love rain down on fragile minds. The result? Nobody knows what love is, but everyone's a fucking expert on what it should be. I don't want to hear about "sacred, unshakable" parental love. If it were so natural, there wouldn't be so many miserable people with crushed self-esteem, told as kids they're nobody, ungrateful beasts, "everyone has normal kids, but you're an idiot," "mom slaves for you, slacker," or the classic "I'm ashamed of you" (almost everyone's got a version of this in their memory, though parents rarely get creative here).

I think all addictions—alcoholism, drugs, gambling, extreme sports, smoking, religious fanaticism—stem from one cause: "life isn't how it should be." It won't bend to match lofty ideals. Shitty reality refuses to change.

Back to love. It's no rocket science. Someone meets someone, falls in love, moves in, yada yada—holy pliers, turns out the person's not the ideal they pretended to be (idealization happens both ways: one tries to be the ideal, the other sees their ideal instead of a real person, otherwise they'd rarely connect). Then everyone's to blame, everything's shit, divorce, kids in therapy, mortgage fucked, "incompatible personalities." :) What a loooove... For whom, exactly?

There's a twist too. After enough bruises, someone might seek what love is and how to do it right. They fall into another trap: "how it should really be." "Love selflessly, jealousy's bad, be a beacon of goodness, blah blah." They think they've cracked it, strive to be that beacon, ban jealousy, bust their ass to change the outside instead of the inside.

It doesn't fucking work.

Because it's still not how it should be. Eventually, they hear you must "love yourself." So our hero (often heroine) dives into self-love. To "love yourself," they read how it's done, get an idea of how a self-loving person should act, and try hard to match that concept.

Does anyone else see this as a massive, endless, impassable shit-show? :)

Here's the kicker: this shitshow applies to me too. When I stumbled on books urging surrender and capitulation, a small, angry part of me screamed that it's bullshit for weaklings, because life's about fighting. I know how it's supposed to be...

The trick, I think, is to surrender to life itself and acknowledge what "shouldn't" exist. Capitulate to your anger, envy, "vices" (mostly deemed so by mommy or other childhood figures). In January, I was in Montañita, a rasta resort in Ecuador. I don't do drugs, but it's a fun spot. There, I tried surfing. The hardest, most annoying part for me was getting into the water, wading to where you wait for waves. With decent waves, it's like "fucked-up life" for many—fighting waves that want to smack your face, sometimes with your own board. You jump, dive, contort to reach the spot.

Then comes capitulation. The same waves stop being obstacles and become a source of joy. The waves don't change—they're the same. They don't give a shit what I think they should be. I might want them to vanish when I enter and appear when I'm ready to ride. They're either there or not. They come in one bottle.
You can't do shit about it. That's all folks.

***

Where Did Patriarchy Come From?

Patriarchy isn't a cultural tradition or a form of family organization. It's a system of power distribution, codified legally, culturally, and economically. It didn't arise naturally—it was formalized, affirmed, and normalized. One of the earliest, clearest sources is the Code of Hammurabi, where women are treated not as subjects but as objects of rights. Not as persons but as property. Their actions—sexual, reproductive, familial—are regulated as if they're assets transferred between men.

The Code's articles state explicitly: if a woman cheats, she can be thrown into the river. If a husband suspects her, his word suffices. If a father decides to marry off his daughter, her consent isn't required. If a woman's behavior is "improper," she faces punishment. But if a man causes harm, it's not a crime. This is structural entrenchment: men are subjects, women are objects of regulation. Even in morality and "duty," men have the right to act, women the obligation to comply.

This principle is reproduced at every level: from religious edicts to modern cultural patterns. Women must be "decent," "predictable," "loyal," "devoted." Men just need to "be men." They can be absent, cheat, be aggressive, or irresponsible—it's all seen as permissible. Women aren't allowed such leeway. They must be reliable, caring, forgiving, endlessly adaptable. The system thus redistributes not just responsibility but the very possibility of deviation.

Modern patriarchy hasn't vanished—it's just changed its language. It's no longer about "obedience" but "femininity." Not "duty to a husband" but "inner wisdom." Women aren't told outright to submit—they're told to be flexible, accept male nature, inspire, not compete, be soft. Under the guise of "self-development," they're programmed for behavioral loyalty. Non-compliance doesn't bring legal punishment but stigma, devaluation, isolation, accusations of "toxicity," "demandingness," "unfemininity."

Patriarchy isn't just domination—it's a system where any female autonomy is a threat. Smart? Dangerous. Independent? Inconvenient. Strong? "Man in a skirt." Sex without attachment? "Cheap." Single? "Nobody wants her." The idea that a woman can be whole without male validation undermines the patriarchal structure. So, culture convinces women they need someone to have the right to exist.

This isn't about personal relationships—it's about systemic power architecture. If nobody dictates who you love or marry today, it doesn't mean the system's gone. It's just more sophisticated. It no longer demands submission—it embeds it in behavioral norms, language, rhetoric, values, even "liberation" narratives. Dismantling patriarchy isn't fighting men—it's tearing down the structure that makes women conditional, judged, and perpetually indebted.

A subdued woman isn't just a matter of power over one person—it's strategic control over the system's reproduction. A broken woman becomes its transmitter. She raises kids within the same norms. She doesn't just pass on genetics—she relays the architecture of submission, embedded in emotional reactions, intonations, expectations, phrases, and interpretations. This is why the system cares not about female freedom but her loyalty. Because women determine whether the next generation will see the world as a fixed order or a living reality where freedom is possible.

We're On A Different Scale
September 12, 2012
Location: BsAs
Music: Moon-Silvered Clouds - Deuter

I've been skimming my friends' feed again and stumbled on Kat's post about how women's independence stops men from being men. They, the bitches, sharpen their own knives and fetch their own coats.

Here's what I've got to say about that.

I don't march in feminist parades or anything—I generally don't like any parades at all. To put it short: I can fetch my own coat, pay for my own dinner, and handle a ton of life's necessities myself.

Guess men's imaginations—or knowledge, skills, talents—don't stretch further. You can totally feel like a badass alpha male with me by, say, playing Chopin on the piano. Or showing me Saturn through a telescope. Or we could talk about how Kant and Plato got it wrong. Trash Aristotle. Mock Nietzsche. Take me sailing. Blow something up, if all else fails.

The only catch is, that takes some brainpower. But everyone wants to feel manly on the cheap. Handing over a coat doesn't take much brain, does it? :)

***

Deconstructing "Femininity"

In modern culture, femininity is sold as a natural, desirable expression of female essence. In reality, it's a constructed behavioral model designed to adapt women to the system's needs. It doesn't arise spontaneously—it's shaped through praise, punishment, cultural archetypes, shaming, language, and expectations. From childhood, girls are taught that being "feminine" means being soft, polite, beautiful, caring, modest, emotionally restrained, and approval-oriented. Anything beyond these bounds is labeled "crude," "inappropriate," "mannish," or "difficult."

The system enforces the "proper woman" as someone who doesn't argue, interrupt, insist, complain, but listens, supports, inspires, and is "easy to talk to." This image supposedly fosters harmony. In practice, it ensures suppression. A woman embedded in this script suppresses anger, swallows disagreement, learns to stomach humiliation, and eventually doesn't notice her subjectivity being erased. Her actions become reactions to external expectations, not inner intuition. Her speech mimics approved lexicon. Her appearance answers the demand to "be pleasing." Her goals aren't desires but attempts to fit in.

Femininity as a code is a disciplinary tool. Under the guise of self-realization, women are pushed to hone service skills. Under "spiritual growth," to more subtly align with a partner's desires. Under "inner strength," to stay composed when boundaries are crossed. Any step outside the template is a personal flaw: too loud, too active, too independent, too cold, too sensitive—always "too much." Women are taught their nature is compliance, and anything non-compliant is deviance.

Men face an equally rigid but status-dominant template: be strong, rational, assertive, emotionally distant, sexually active, controlling. Deviations—vulnerability, softness, doubt, needing validation—are weakness, punished by stigma. Men's freedom, though, is confined to their functional role: they can vary, but only within a range that keeps them controllers. Women are denied even this sliver of freedom, as their role is status-subordinate. They're relegated to regulated objects, not active subjects. Both genders are funneled into strict role corridors: men obligated to control, women to comply. This is the manipulative core: men can be varied; women are either "feminine" or "wrong." Femininity isn't a spectrum, freedom, or expression—it's a disciplinary role demanding endless self-control, aesthetic pressure, and behavioral loyalty.

Being Unhomely Is Awful :)

November 15, 2010
Location: Baños
Music: News - Dire Straits

One thing I've been chewed out for most in life (besides drinking, smoking, and swearing like a sailor) is my so-called "unhomeliness." My loathing for domestic chores, that is. I've hated cleaning, laundry, cooking, and dishwashing since childhood and never really did them, earning a low-prestige slob reputation. People tried to brainwash me, saying, "If you don't mop the floor, no one'll marry you." That baffled me—if "marriage" is like signing up to be a maid, why the fuck would I want it?

At 17, I bailed from Novosibirsk to live alone in Moscow. Having accepted my messy rep and being cool with being a lazy pig who only breeds filth, I didn't try hard to keep order or run a household. I was convinced I was utterly hopeless at it and would never manage.

Still, I had to do something—when breathing dust got old or the last clean plate joined the Tetris stack in the sink, I'd make a cosmic effort and spend a day making the place tolerable. That's how sad, unshaven bachelors live :) Frozen dumplings, boxed cutlets, beer, bottle armies under the table, overflowing ashtrays, and the cigarette smoke so thick you could hang an axe in it.

When a new relationship with some guy started, I'd initially try to hide my slob side, cleaning ten times more often, cooking "homely" stuff, acting like a "normal person." The promo lasted a month or two. Then the homemaker role smoothly shifted to the guy, with no real options.

Oh, I learned to cook earlier, for a simple reason—I traveled to exotic places, fell in love with their food, and went to restaurants so often I wanted to make tasty stuff at home, cheaper, and in a giant bowl, why skimp? So, I cook pretty fucking awesomely sometimes, purely creative, usually without recipes (I check for new dishes to get the gist). Cooking's stayed creative for me, never a chore.

By the time I got to Baños, my domestic enlightenment had peaked—I could keep the apartment tidy almost always. A new suitor helped, not wanting to look like a slob, but it felt natural and easy. Then the landlords offered weekly full cleaning for an extra $20 a month.

Now, I do fuck-all. I still cook when inspired, but my only chores (besides occasional dishwashing when clean ones run out before cleaning day) are calling the laundry service to pick up my clothes and not forgetting to open the gate 2-3 hours later to grab the clean stuff and pay. My poor head was drilled with the idea that life's harsh, you must slave daily at chores to avoid being a lazy pig unworthy of respect. And mop the floor, always mop the damn floor.

I also love tossing stuff everywhere. I've got a floor stash of blankets, throws, and pillows to lounge on, and if I come home drunk on a Saturday, my jacket, pants, and socks join the pile, creating glorious chaos. For the maid, I've got a special quest: "Find all the beer bottles in the corners."

They wasted their time chewing me out. This fabled "homeliness" isn't worth shit. If you want, you can live like this just fine. As for "no one'll marry you"—fuck it, I'm not aiming there anyway.

The Stanford Experiment and Role-Based Submission

One of the most vivid empirical confirmations of systemic role-based submission is the Stanford Prison Experiment, conducted by Philip Zimbardo in 1971. Its aim was simple: simulate a prison environment, randomly assigning volunteers as guards or prisoners. All were equal, all knew it was an experiment. Yet, within days, guards began showing cruelty, while prisoners displayed anxiety, compliance, and loss of agency.

The experiment's key insight isn't that "people can be cruel" but that role structures produce behavior. No one trained participants to be sadistic or submissive. But once a system granted some power and required others to obey, transformation began. Behavior shifted not due to personal traits but due to role context. Participants played roles, yet faced real psychological and behavioral consequences, as if the roles were reality.

Zimbardo halted the experiment early due to participants' genuine psychological breakdown. The takeaway: create a structure and assign roles, and the system will shape behavior on its own. Domination and submission aren't personal traits —they're functional outcomes of the architecture. This is why patriarchy, as a hierarchical system, automatically produces suppression without needing individual malice. It's enough for one subject to have interpretive power and another to be obligated to comply.

The Stanford Experiment shows why "not all men are like that" misses the point in systemic analysis. The issue isn't individual attitudes but a role structure that predetermines behavior through power access. Just as a "good" person can turn aggressive as a guard, a man embedded in patriarchal norms will reproduce the system, even unconsciously—not because he's evil, but because he's privileged to not see the subordinate as an equal subject.

This is why freedom can't exist within "good relationships." The system doesn't need cruelty—it needs role compliance. If a relationship has hierarchy—where one stays silent for peace and the other sees it as normal—the system is at work. It doesn't require overt violence. The architecture is enough.

Reproductive Violence

Reproductive violence isn't an aberration but a built-in mechanism of the patriarchal system. It starts long before conception and isn't limited to physical coercion. It's the imposed notion of female destiny, cultural blackmail via "maternal duty," family pressure, childlessness stigma, and the myth that a woman's biological fulfillment requires childbirth. This is a structure that doesn't offer motherhood as an option but mandates it as the default path. Choosing not to reproduce demands justification, proof, explanation, while choosing to reproduce is seen as self-evident, needing no argument.

The violence lies in the norm, not direct orders. Women aren't told, "You must reproduce." They're asked, "When are you starting?" "Your clock's ticking," "A woman fulfills herself through motherhood." She can be talented, smart, independent, but without fitting the "wife-mother" script, she's incomplete. Society doesn't see her as whole. Her maturity is deemed partial. Even medicine reinforces this: gynecological norms assume future pregnancy. A woman's body is treated as a temporary vessel for a fetus, not an autonomous system.

The system denies women the right to not want. It pretends this is her choice. That's the violence: when only one script is permissible but sold as freedom. Women are "allowed" not to reproduce only with excuses—health issues, "it didn't work out," "no suitable partner," "career." None acknowledge the core: I don't want to. I'm not obligated. I don't owe anyone. In a society where women are reproductive units, opting out is a flaw.

When a woman reproduces not from desire but because "it's time," "age pressure," "mom insists," "to keep the husband," or "it's expected," that's systemic violence's result. The child becomes her legitimacy in the system's eyes, not her choice. Then, she's demanded to show unconditional love, engagement, and sacrifice. If she falters, she's a "bad mother." The system imposes the role, then punishes imperfect performance.

Reproductive violence also manifests in medical paternalism: denying sterilization, pushing unwanted pregnancies, dismissing pain or anxiety, framing dissent as hysteria or shortsightedness. When a woman's body is seen as collective property, her agency is secondary—or nonexistent.

Exposing this isn't about "to reproduce or not." It's about the right to be human beyond function. To decide without explanation. To have a body that belongs to neither state, partner, family, culture, nor demographics. If that right isn't recognized, the violence hasn't ended—it's just changed form.

On Clothing
September 30, 2011
Location: BsAs

Those who know me probably have a decent idea of my clothing style. Jeans, T-shirts, sneakers. Comfortable, practical, versatile. Some old acquaintances might remember me in sexy shorts and on high heels, rocking some provocative tops, but let's not dig up my darketh past. Back then, I genuinely thought I was hideous but desperately wanted to believe in something better, so I leaned into that flashy sexuality to prop up my limping self-esteem.

Friends, both guys and girls, occasionally nag me about my sloppy wardrobe. From one side or another, I get hit with advice like, "For fuck's sake, start dressing more feminine, you look like a dude, nothing shows under those T-shirts and shirts, blah-blah-blah." From the other ear, two at once: "You've got stuff to show off, but you hide it, how can you live like thaaaat?"

I twist myself into knots trying to explain. Look, boys and girls, the thing is, I don't want to spark sexual fantasies in every random passerby. After nearly two years in Ecuador, I'm fucking exhausted from the drooling dogs circling me, publicly slobbering and trying to drag me to bed five minutes after meeting, barely learning my name.

In Russia, there wasn't this frenzy. As a kid, I dreamed—like in the movies—of waking up one day as Princess Swan. Well, it came true, to my detriment: in Ecuador's cultural context, I landed in the category of pale-skinned, blue-eyed exoticism, deemed beautiful by default, even if you're a lopsided cow. And off it went.

At first, it was kind of fun. So much attention out of nowhere, ooooh... and they're all falling over themselves, pick whoever you want. Later, I realized the choice was like a Chinese market—tons of stuff, dirt cheap, but the quality's absolute shit. You didn't even need to sleep with them to figure it out; five minutes of talking or just watching from the sidelines was enough.

Enough lyrical digressions, let's get to the point.

All these talks about "dress like a woman, show your curves" made me think again about the meaning of life—er, I mean, why bother? I've got no matrimonial goals, I'm not rushing to pop out kids, and screwing randoms is even less my thing. So, there's zero pleasure in having every guy around me drooling with their tongues out.

There's a theory that women dress not for men but for each other. That's always been beyond me, like something from another dimension, outside my experience or imagination. No comment.

But after hearing all these arguments, my amigos still insist I stop hiding my "insanely gorgeous" body under tacky T-shirts with Latin phrases like "Stercus Accidit" ("Shit Happens"). Sometimes, I even think they might have a point. But the second I step out in, say, shorts, leggings, and a tight tank top, I'm nauseated by the neck-craning punks, syrupy comments from all sides, and the silent hatred from women in my line of sight. Fuck, where's the thrill in that?

Sometimes I wonder if I've got a superiority complex or I'm just too picky. I'm not against showing off this proverbial Body—but to someone I choose. Maybe even without all these rags.

Psychologists explain this behavior in women as a childhood-rooted dependency: their self-esteem hinges on how many guys lust after them. So, they constantly try to up that number to feel more like an alpha female. I played those games too, but I'm done with them. I've grown a bit, and I don't quite see myself as a "female" anymore. I dare to hope I've evolved slightly from animal to sapiens, and picked up some epic self-assurance along the way. I don't really need others' worship to feel good—honestly, it embarrasses me, since I know the flip side of that coin.

Fuck, I keep losing my train of thought... Where was I? Oh, right.

About Ecuador. They've got these macho types, you know. He wants you, and you, the bitch, tell him ~~"go fuck yourself"~~—er, "no." He gets offended, starts bombarding you with texts, gets jealous of everyone for no reason, throws tantrums like he's been your husband for a decade, and so on. Doesn't exactly spark enthusiasm.

So, whoever wants to show off, let them, if they've got something to show. I'll stick to my jeans, T-shirts, and Diesel. I don't shy away from perfume or makeup—I'm a pro at those. It's probably a funny combo: expensive (sometimes really expensive) perfume, near-professional makeup, ratty sneakers, and a baggy T-shirt saying, like, "Times New Roman - the boring font."

...Though sometimes I sit and think—maybe, just maybe, something's wrong with me?! o_O

***

Parenting as a Systemic Tool

Parenting, within the system, isn't an act of love or self-extension—it's a tool for reproducing norms. It's embedded in the cultural architecture as a mandatory life stage and a mechanism for passing role templates to the next generation. In the patriarchal and disciplinary model, parenting becomes a form of social programming, where "upbringing" is essentially training for integration into the same structures that suppress the parents themselves.

A child isn't seen as an autonomous subject but as raw material. Their feelings are deemed "unformed," their desires "whims," their resistance "disobedience." A parent, lacking experience of freedom, can't impart it—they transmit control. They teach the child not to live but to adapt, not to understand themselves but to conform, not to discern reality but to guess expectations. Often, they genuinely believe this is love.

This is the system's sophistication: parenting is framed as duty, love, care, but functions as discipline. The more suppressed the parent, the stricter they enforce rules. The more anxious they are, the more they demand obedience. They can't handle a child's freedom because they've never known it themselves. Taught to fear mistakes, comparison, judgment, exclusion, they pass that fear forward, even unintentionally.

The cultural model of a "good parent" is a disciplining overseer wrapped in love. It's not enough to care—you must raise. Set boundaries, shape behavior, uphold norms. The system doesn't allow parents to be living humans alongside living children—it demands they be functions. Thus, every parent becomes a system's relay, either enforcing "how it should be" or struggling against themselves, with no alternative model to lean on.

Refusing systemic parenting isn't rejecting children—it's rejecting the false script where a child is a tool for self-validation, an insurance against loneliness, or a badge of cultural legitimacy. A child isn't a function, project, or extension—they're a separate person with their own trajectory, not obligated to affirm anyone's worth. Without access to their own freedom, a parent can't support another's—they'll reproduce the system, even unwillingly.

The system doesn't want free children. They're inconvenient, they see through falsity, they ask questions. So, training starts early—"don't yell," "don't interrupt," "don't be angry," "don't talk nonsense." This is early normalization, aiming to make the child convenient. Then, they're funneled into hierarchy: school, grades, discipline, career, adaptation. Without deconstructing themselves, parents inevitably conduct this cycle.

Breaking free is possible when parenting ceases to be a function and becomes a relationship—not a template, but a living interaction. Boundaries aren't imposed but co-created. The adult doesn't assert control but stays present—not to raise, but to be. Only then can the system's generational transmission be interrupted.

Manipulation, Narcissism, and Pickup

Manipulation isn't a deviation in the system—it's the norm, embedded in language, behavior, and interaction culture. This is stark in romantic relationships, where narcissistic dynamics are sold as attractiveness and abusive behavior as passion or charisma. A man playing hot-and-cold, creating attention scarcity, ghosting then returning with feigned interest, isn't seen as an aggressor—he's "captivating," "mysterious," "a man to understand." Women are scripted to decode, retain, be "interesting enough," "not pushy," "not heavy."

This dynamic is systemically useful: it makes women manageable, anxious, and dependent on validation. Pickup culture formalized this into an ideology. Ignoring, devaluing, keeping distance, showing interest in other women, criticizing "excessive emotionality"—these became "seduction" techniques. In essence, they're domination and boundary-breaking tactics. The goal: create scarcity, shifting a woman's focus from her needs to his. She stops asking, "Is this person right for me?" and starts asking, "What can I do to make him want me?" This isn't courtship—it's embedding a subordinate role.

Narcissism here isn't a diagnosis but a systemic adaptation. A person who mimics interest, maintains an illusion of closeness, yet remains emotionally unavailable and insensitive to others' boundaries, is valued because this model serves the system. It reproduces inequality, making the other doubt themselves, chase, justify, stay vulnerable. This is called "love," "challenging relationships," "karmic attraction," but it's emotional abuse dressed as passion.

Manipulation thrives on removing clarity. Don't say someone's unwanted—ghost them. Don't explain disinterest—stir jealousy. Don't address pain—blame "overreaction." This creates a systemic loop: someone anxious and confused stays in the system, hoping "it'll work out." They don't leave because there's no clear rejection. In this ambiguity, the manipulator gains full control—they promise nothing but demand everything, guarantee nothing but evoke duty, do no overt harm but leave the other in cognitive paralysis.

The system normalizes this. Under "female wisdom," women are told to endure, "not dramatize," "understand his tough phase," "be soft," "give space." A woman calling this abuse is mocked as hysterical, feminist, bitter, or bad at "building relationships." This is the system's defense—it doesn't want manipulation named. Naming it would force rethinking the order where ignoring and power are normal, and emotional honesty is weakness.

There's no mystery, no "complex personalities," no "special stories." There's only behavior that violates boundaries. Freedom begins not with psychology but with deconstructing language. Call it passion, and you're trapped. Call it dynamics, and you lose. Think you can "earn" love, and you're playing the system's rules. You'll never escape a context where the manipulator is always right, because the system gave them carte blanche.

Raising and Normalizing Children

Socializing children in the system isn't nurturing—it's formatting to fit the norm. From their earliest years, children are immersed in a dense field of cultural prescriptions, not framed as overt violence but embedded in language, cartoons, adult tones, behaviors, rewards, and punishments. The child doesn't learn to be themselves—they learn to anticipate. They quickly grasp that certain emotions are "unacceptable," certain desires "shameful," certain questions "silly." They're not given a map of reality but a map of what's approved.

This map is narrow. It leaves no room for spontaneity, depth, doubt, or resistance. The child isn't told why they're suppressed—just that they're "too sensitive," "too loud," "inconvenient." Their personal boundaries form not from within but from external sanctions. As a result, they don't know where their true self lies—only how to be approved.

This creates a fundamental rift: between what the child feels and what they can express. This rift is the core of systemic suppression, fostering lifelong inner unfreedom. First, children are taught "don't throw tantrums," "don't embarrass us," "don't argue with adults." Then, "don't show off," "don't act too smart," "don't stand out." Later, "think about your future," "build a career," "start a family." None of this is their choice—it's the system's continuation, disguised as "care for the child."

The family is the primary transmitter of norms. It shapes the language through which the child later perceives themselves and the world: conditional love ("you're great when..."), constant evaluation ("why not an A?"), shame ("aren't you ashamed?"), fear ("don't do that, you'll get in trouble"). This language is absorbed before the child understands words. It's not the parents' individual fault—it's the structure. They were raised in the same code and pass it on as "common sense."

School reinforces the programming: discipline, obedience, hierarchy, fear of mistakes, craving approval. Cartoons add gender roles, "good behavior" models, and the idea that rewards come only from compliance. Fairy tales introduce binary logic: good vs. bad, right vs. wrong, saved vs. punished. It's sold as "personality formation," but it's the dismantling of everything alive.

By adulthood, people no longer know where their true desires end and programming begins. They fear being themselves because it's risky. They weren't taught to be—they were taught to fit in. Even self-proclaimed "rebels" often just flip the signs, staying in the same logic: not "I want" but "I'm not like them." Not freedom, but reverse dependence on the same coordinates.

Breaking this starts with language. As long as parents say, "don't cry," "be good," "everyone does it," "that's how it's done," they're not raising a person—they're programming a norm-carrier. Freedom begins where a child has the right to be themselves, no caveats. Where their feelings aren't explained away, dismissed, or interpreted. Where the parent doesn't judge but accompanies. This isn't a method—it's a way of existing outside the system. Anything else is passing on violence under the guise of upbringing.

Making Dreams Come True?
July 11, 2009
Music: I Don't Want To Be - Gavin DeGraw

As a kid, my slogan was, "I do what I want."

Adults didn't like that, probably because they'd long abandoned such "unacceptable luxury." I couldn't wrap my head around it—why the hell did most grown-ups around me keep doing shit they clearly hated, yelling from all directions: "There's this word—'must'" as if it explained everything? Looking at them, growing up seemed like the last thing I wanted.

And I couldn't figure out the point of it all. If you have to force yourself to go to school every damn day, just to go to college every damn day, just to go to work every damn day... that prospect was so bleak, I couldn't see what it was all for.

***

The Family System as a Cradle of Shame

The collective family system isn't just a group of relatives—it's a structure where the kin functions as a channel for transmitting norms, embedded in horizontal and vertical relationships. There are no subjects here, only roles: daughter, wife, son-in-law, grandmother, aunt. These aren't just statuses—they're expected behaviors. When someone deviates, the system activates pressure mechanisms, from devaluation to outright violence.

This system doesn't need overt aggression. Its tool is shame, wielded through comparison, silence, exclusion, and blame. Phrases like "you can't treat your mother like that," "what will the neighbors say," "you're shaming the family" aren't mere remarks—they're directives to restore hierarchy. Preserving the illusion of normalcy trumps acknowledging reality. Violence can stay hidden for years because open discussion is disloyalty. Breaking the facade is betrayal.

The system's strength is its self-reproduction. Even those who suffered its rules as children often revert to its logic as adults. Recognition in this system requires compliance. A good daughter doesn't argue. A good wife endures. A good son provides. A good parent "keeps things in the family." It's built on roles, not reality. Even victims of violence are expected to conform.

Collective upbringing operates like an army. Relatives become overseers, interpreters, judges. Your feelings are discussed behind your back, your choices criticized, your autonomy a threat. Officially, it's "care." Resistance is ingratitude, distance is betrayal, independence is deviance. Even if you move to another continent, the structure lingers as an internal censor, asking systemic questions: "Am I doing this right?" "What will they think?" "Can I do this?"

The family structure isn't a person—it's a code. It speaks through grandma's voice, lives in recipes, holidays, photo albums. It shows in compliments and reproaches, pity and demands. It mirrors patriarchal norms, but in a more intimate, enveloping form. Its power lies in collective silent agreement: if you step out, you shatter the shared reality. That threatens the system, as your exit exposes its artificiality.

Breaking free often means breaking with part of the family—not always physically, but logically. It's refusing to live by others' scales, to seek permission, justify, or conform. Not because you're selfish, but because you see: loyalty to a system where love exists only for silence and submission isn't love—it's a format. To exit, you must reject being "good" by their metrics, even if it costs status, kinship, or understanding. You choose yourself—not as a role, but as a living person.

Shame and Disgrace

May 19, 2010

To all newly arrived friends, I'm semi-mandatorily proposing you share your most utterly shameful life story. If you've got the guts, hehe. :) Has anything ever happened to you that made you break out in a cold sweat, leaving you with one desperate wish

—to vanish without a trace right then and there, sink through the floor, or at least rewind one day to avoid that disgrace? :)

I'll go first.

Once, when I was really little (I don't recall exactly, maybe around five), my mother and I visited one of her friends who, by chance, had a son about my age. While the grown-up aunties chatted, we were sent to the kid's room, and the boy (I don't even remember his name) started showing me... no, not what you're thinking, just his toy collection.
While ogling the boy's treasure trove, I stumbled upon a little box. And found a fortune inside. One Ruble. As I recall, the decision didn't take long. Money, as we know, doesn't stink, and a ruble for a five-year-old in the mid-80s was at least 5 to 10 scoops of ice cream. Sure, I vaguely knew stealing was bad, but somehow that word didn't connect to the act in my mind. So, I decided to... just take it.

It would've ended fine if not for my blabbermouth, which got me in trouble with my parents more than once. Either I flashed my loot or, in some blissful burst of honesty, spilled the beans to my mother. Either way, I got caught, and in a really dumb way. Epic fail.

My memory refuses to dredge up the details of the shitstorm that followed, but I was dragged back to that same friend's place, under the arm, to return the stolen goods. I tried for ages to explain to my mother that borrowing isn't the same as stealing, and that mixing up concepts leads to such harsh consequences. Nothing worked.

Honestly, that story didn't teach me much. Because later, in music school, we merrily rummaged through coat pockets in the cloakroom (in that temple of music!) and nicked loose change and sunflower seeds while the sweet old lady guarding the young talents' stuff dozed over some literary masterpiece.

Myths About Love and "Female Happiness"

The ideology of love in mass consciousness isn't a description of a living feeling but a construct designed to keep people in a system of dependency and repetition. Myths about "soulmates," "destiny," and "female happiness" as life's goal aren't romantic—they're disciplinary tools. So deeply embedded in culture that they're taken as truth, they serve a clear function: make solitude suspicious, relationships mandatory, and suffering legitimate.

The soulmate myth claims a person is inherently incomplete, needing another half to be whole. This fundamental distortion, woven into language and cultural imagery, pathologizes solitude. Any connection, even a toxic one, is seen as better than none. This setup makes people vulnerable to emotional, material, or psychological dependency, as they're taught from the start: you're not complete without another.

The myth of love as life's meaning sidesteps the question of meaning itself. It frames suffering for love as depth, and jealousy, pain, or humiliation as proof of authentic feelings, not signs of abuse. It swaps freedom for belonging, individuality for dissolution, respect for endurance. In this logic, healthy distance is impossible: anything less than consuming is "cold," anything without drama "not real enough." Anxiety and dependency are sold as markers of sincerity.

The myth of female happiness through family and children is a cultural program. A woman who doesn't follow this script is automatically labeled "unfulfilled." Her status is questioned, no matter her path. Even if she's accomplished, free, and healthy, she's hit with: "Why are you alone?" "Don't you want kids?" "You must be tough to deal with." These aren't questions—they're compliance checks. Their goal isn't inquiry but to nudge her back into the normative corridor, where a woman's value lies in being wanted, not in her autonomy.

In the logic of systemic control, love isn't a feeling but a structure—a script of roles, duties, expectations, emotional investments, and social approval. The "everything's fine" benchmark boils down to signs: living together, having kids, no public scandals. The system doesn't ask, "Are we happy?" It asks, "Do we look normal?" This cultural framework excludes subjectivity. Those who don't fit are deemed inadequate, not the system flawed.

Dismantling these myths doesn't mean rejecting love—it means rejecting its counterfeit. Love doesn't require dissolution, proof, pain, or social validation. It isn't more valuable with suffering or void without partnership. Intimacy needs no norms, permission, or templates. Its only condition is being yourself without losing that right beside another.

On Luv

August 21, 2009
Music: This Guitar (Can't Keep) - George Harrison

Here's the thing: people tend to attach some weird significance to the words "I love you." From what I've seen, they're rarely taken literally. Instead, they're a code for something else—"I'm dependent on you," "now you owe me," "I want to be with you forever," "I want you to love me," or, hell, "I really want to screw you."

For most, these words are wrapped in this insane aura of importance, some fucking exclusivity. It's hilarious when serious dudes who "don't toss those words around lightly" mock girls waiting for princes on white horses—because, honestly, it's pretty much the same thing.

I can't shake the feeling that people who believe they can only have one great love in life (okay, maybe two or three) don't actually know how to love. If you know how to love, you know it's a resource you can't exhaust or limit. It's like saying, "I'll only eat oranges my whole life, loyal to them till I die." Stupid as hell.

It hit me that the kind of love people make exclusive has nothing to do with actual love. Love is pretty ordinary, natural stuff. It's like saying, "I'll only breathe when I'm with you, otherwise I'm holding my breath." That's half-death, if you ask me.
But people, damn it, crave exclusivity. Everything just for me, and screw everyone else. It's like trying to lock up the air.

****

Transmission of the System Across Generations

The system couldn't survive without its ability to reproduce. Its greatest strength lies not in overt violence but in subtle transmission—not in explicit dictates but in normalization. Each generation passes the system forward unconsciously—through language, intonations, daily actions, facial expressions, instinctive reactions. This keeps the system alive: not as an external demand but as an internal programming, perceived as one's own.

The system isn't transmitted through content but through form. It's embedded in fairy tales, responses to emotions, pedagogical remarks, casual speech, jokes, "polite" gestures. It's reinforced not by instructions but by repeated patterns. What a child sees as permissible, they adopt. What's deemed "natural," they don't question. This is the system's power—it needs no defense because it's built into the way we interact.

Breaking free requires recognizing the structure. As long as someone sees anxiety as a personality trait, shame as a sign of conscience, or compliance as good manners, they stay trapped. Until they discern what was implanted, they pass it on. Even if they swear, "I'll never be like them." Even if they think they're "doing it differently."

Transmission can disguise itself as care, responsibility, or "wanting the best." But if fear, control, and conformity still lurk behind it, the outcome is the same. The system lives not in words but in the logic of relationships. Without changing that logic, there's only reproduction—in new guises, with new words, but the same structure. The only way to break the chain is to refuse to pass on the old, even without knowing what comes next. The key is to stop the automatic repetition disguised as care.

Eureka

July 20, 2011
Location: BsAs
Music: Rondo for Two Pianos in C Major, Op. 73 - Chopin, Frederic

This divine music playing right now led me to a mind-blowing revelation. It hit me crystal clear how they deliberately turned us into idiots since childhood.
At least, they did it to me. And they succeeded.

Around age four, when I learned to use the record player, I eventually got sick of listening to The Blue Puppy, which, by the way, was awesome in its own right. I moved on to classical music. Mozart's Lacrimosa from the Requiem blew my mind. We didn't have the full Requiem on vinyl, I think, because otherwise I'd have been obsessed with Introitus, Domine Jesu, and Lux Aeterna too—those are just insanely fucking incredible.

Then I went to kindergarten, where bossy, dumb, smug teachers thought all kids should act like kids and not "show off."

They made us idiotically march in circles to shitty renditions of questionable round-dance tunes, singing stuff like "A Christmas Tree Was Born in the Forest" (Russian equivalent of "Twinkle Twinkle Little Star" or "Frosty the Snowman"). It was unbearable. I felt like a moron. What the fuck kind of Christmas tree after Lacrimosa? They turned my brain upside down.

I figured it was probably better to blend in, to avoid getting whacked on the head with annoying regularity. So, for almost 30 years, I tried to be like everyone else, thinking I must be crazy.

Then, in music school, they shoved classical masterpieces down our throats the wrong way. It was too late, and besides, you can't do it like that—it's a surefire way to breed disgust instead of love. Only now do I grasp the full vileness of this violence against the human soul. Forcing someone to listen to—or worse, perform!—beauty under duress steals their chance to ever truly enjoy it. They didn't make me hate it; I had an inoculation. But they did tear me away from it. One tiny hook remained—my piano teacher, who was obsessed with Bach, infected me too, thank God. But it was a drop in the bucket.

They told us, lazy dimwits, that we'd never grow up to appreciate high art.
Go to hell, I'd say now—we're born with that appreciation. There's nothing to "understand." It's just beautiful, inherently awesome, no explanation needed. At four, a person can take in any masterpiece because they don't try to analyze it—they just hear, see, and feel it.

The scale of it is staggering. The scale of the nastiness that stole my classical music for 25 years. Now I'm sitting here, downloading gigabytes of it—Chopin, Mozart, Beethoven, Bach, Brahms, all of it—and devouring it like someone who hasn't eaten in 25 years.

What a fucking mess, just think about it.

***

Approval of Others as a Tool of Control

"Better to be a good person with a dirty mouth than a quiet, well-mannered asshole."
— Faina Ranevskaya

Fake Politeness

The phrase "how are you?" isn't a question—it's a ritual. It doesn't expect an answer, doesn't demand engagement, and carries no genuine interest. It's a social signal, the equivalent of a button saying, "I'm normal, you're normal, don't bother me." The structure of everyday politeness isn't about empathy—it's about maintaining external smoothness. It's not designed for understanding. It's designed for masking.

The system has built ritualized forms of communication where meaning doesn't matter—form does. You're not taught to hear another person; you're taught to act like you care. Not to show involvement, but to display a socially approved reaction. In this setup, politeness becomes a convenient cover for emotional indifference. You don't have to care—you just have to look proper.

Genuine empathy requires time, resources, openness. It's vulnerable. That makes it inefficient for a system invested in reproducing masks. The system doesn't need living interactions—it needs people to stay within the ritual. To know when to smile, say "nice to meet you," agree, yield, or compliment. This isn't about ethics—it's about training. The better you've mastered this training, the more "well-mannered" you're deemed. In reality, the more submissive to the structure of external compliance.

Even a simple "hello" in the system's paradigm isn't a greeting—it's a test. Did you say it? Did you forget? Are you following the code? Did you respond correctly? Not too coldly? Not too warmly? This isn't conversation—it's an audit of behavioral loyalty. You're not a person; you're a cog in the social interface.

This is why genuinely direct people are often seen as rude, confrontational, or "off." They break the script. They say it like it is. They didn't learn the proper pause between "how are you" and "I'm fine." If they say they're not fine, they breach the contract—because that question isn't for answering. It's for validating normalcy. Any response that disrupts the template triggers anxiety. Anxiety is a system glitch—it's either ignored or punished.

Fake politeness isn't an isolated case—it's a structural code. It starts in childhood: "say thank you," "don't be rude," "smile," "look simpler," "don't sulk," "say hi to aunty." This isn't upbringing—it's the start of unlearning honest existence. For the rest of their lives, people keep playing—at interest, sympathy, approval, being "good." They fear silence, not responding, not smiling back. They've been taught: if you don't play, you're a violator. Even if you're in pain, you must say "everything's fine." Because truth is impolite. And thus, wrong.
But if truth requires breaking the form, maybe the form itself is a lie?

Rules of Behavior as Training

Rules of behavior aren't about comfort—they're about control. They're sold as "good manners," "etiquette," "respect for others," but they function to embed people in a role structure where behavior must match external expectations, not internal states. The system trains you from childhood: don't put elbows on the table, don't talk with your mouth full, don't slurp, don't interrupt, don't laugh loudly, don't ask "stupid" questions. These instructions aren't about respect—their goal is discipline.

From an early age, people are trained not just to eat neatly but to exist under scrutiny. Even eating—a basic bodily function—is subject to cultural constructs. You don't just eat; you must eat "properly." The Soviet canteen slogan, "when I eat, I'm deaf and mute," captures it: the body must be silent, erased from social reality. Even your mouth isn't yours—it must be controlled. Breaking this code isn't seen as a preference but as degradation: "savage," "shame," "disgrace."

This plants the core idea: the body is suspect unless controlled. Desire, voice, facial expressions, gestures, laughter, tears, hunger—all must be regulated. The system can't tolerate bodily spontaneity because it's unmanageable. So, control starts with food, continues in school, solidifies in the office, and invades intimate relationships. The ideal citizen is someone who doesn't break script, even in pain. That's what "proper behavior" teaches.

Any deviation is labeled uncultured, but the norm itself goes unexplained. Why no elbows on the table? Why no loud laughter? There's no answer—just the command: "you can't." Meaning doesn't matter; obedience does. Children aren't taught to understand—they're taught not to violate. Even if it deadens their behavior and automates their reactions.

Etiquette becomes a gatekeeping code: how well someone's sewn into the system, how much they suppress spontaneity, how ready they are to swap the living for the outwardly acceptable. Step outside these bounds, and you're a threat—not because you did wrong, but because you refused the ritual.

You stopped asking how to sit, speak, eat, react. You reclaimed your body. In this logic, that's unforgivable.

That's why you can't just eat at the table. Because the system can't let you just be.

No Word for "Want," Only "Must"

October 18, 2010
Location: Baños
Music: Señal que te he perdido - Andrés Calamaro

I don't know about others, but I heard this phrase constantly as a kid. And it's not easy to realize what utter bullshit it is—capable of turning life into a dull, joyless grind, a life without the faintest clue about your own desires. Because "want" just vanishes, buried under an avalanche of "musts." Must eat, must sleep, must work, must walk, must dress warmly, must hang out with friends, must rest. That's not living—that's complete crap, if you ask me. It kills any pleasure in these simple things. Like that joke:

"—I only eat when I'm hungry...
—God, you're like an animal!"

Here's the truth: there's no such thing as "must." There's only "want." All those "musts" are just garbage.

At home, they didn't force me to eat on a schedule, but that was later, when I was older. Then there was kindergarten, where the food was usually gross, and they weren't above dirty blackmail to make kids eat, even if the smell alone made you gag (I remember these disgusting, revolting fish cutlets, absolute vile stuff). I read someone's charming memory of a teacher threatening to slice open kids' stomachs and stuff the food directly in if they wouldn't eat through their mouths.

Nap time was its own nightmare. I think things like insomnia, "night owls," and other sleep issues owe something to that forced bullshit. I never wanted to nap. I think it's disgusting to make someone sleep when they don't want to. But for those who didn't, they had ways. Don't want to sleep? We'll strip you naked and make you stand in front of everyone, so you're ashamed. Ashamed that your growing body has so much energy it can't just shut down.

And all this was seen as normal. The habit of accepting violence from childhood breeds a habit of self-violence later. There's plenty written on this, but reading books usually changes nothing. There's this thing called "Primal Therapy" by Arthur Janov, wildly popular in the U.S. decades ago. If you know Lennon's story, you probably know he went through it. I read the book, dug around online, and my take is mixed. On one hand, it was a slickly marketed business, and insider reviews suggest its effectiveness was pretty low. But there's a kernel of truth in it, I think: it's not just about recalling childhood traumas but reliving and feeling them again. Alexander Lowen writes about this too, and I vibe with him more because Janov leans too hard into "my therapy is the only way to save yourself" :) That's a big red flag for me.

There was also this popular U.S. training called EST (Erhard Seminars Training), which cleared the mind from a different angle. By the way, there's a decent book on it, Transformation by Luke Rhinehart—check it out online if you're into this stuff :)

A little quote:

"Definitely, one reason sex is so attractive to men and women is that it's one of the few places where enlivening experiences, killed off in almost every other sphere, are still possible. But don't get too excited. Most of you have never fucked. Most of you, assholes, haven't fucked since you were sixteen. I don't care how many beds you've hopped. You're fucking in your head. One

reason assholes chase new partners is they can't get full satisfaction with one person and think maybe they will with twenty."

It's the same with food, I think. For a while, I was obsessed with chasing ever more exotic eats, during a period when money wasn't an issue. It was a search for lost natural pleasure, an attempt to fill a sensory void. And honestly, it was awful. I didn't have any "must eat this, not that" beliefs—my folks spared me that. But tons of people force themselves to choke down "healthy food" that sparks zero joy in their taste buds or gut, only in their brains, because they're eating "for the idea." The original point of food—long forgotten and buried. That's partly why diets are so popular: it's awesome when someone tells you exactly what to eat and when. You're freed from the agonizing need to make your own choices.

And so, many of us know this scene: standing in front of an open fridge, unable to tell if we're hungry. It's easier when someone says, "You must eat"—no problem then, no need to painfully question what you want. I often don't know if I want to eat. Or sleep. Or anything else basic. Yet we wander around chasing grand ideas about the meaning of life, cosmic love, tantric sex, and other lofty crap. It's like trying to build a house after torching the foundation.

A quick word on calls to "love yourself and don't stress." Sounds like another trendy way to screw yourself over. When someone's got a splinter in their ass and they're trying to find and pull it out, people say, "Chill, love yourself, don't sweat it." To me, "loving yourself" is exactly about finding those splinters to stop squirming in pain. Pretending the pain isn't there is just another "how you must live" concept—self-deception and disrespect to your own nature. It's got shades of that brutal "parental love": you feel like shit but can't figure out why because you're disconnected, and they tell you, "You're spoiled, you've got no real problems, stop bitching, go do something useful."

Approval as a Currency of Submission

Approval in the system isn't feedback—it's a way to regulate behavior. It acts as a reward, a marker of belonging, a tool of socialization through dependency. From childhood, a person is taught: do it "right," and you're praised; do it "wrong," and you face withdrawal, punishment, or shame. Reasons aren't explained—behavior is simply labeled "acceptable" or "unacceptable." To avoid sanctions, you learn to guess.

This forms a core belief: your worth isn't who you are but how much you're approved of. It creates false subjectivity—you exist not as yourself but through the lens of external reactions. Even as an adult, someone raised in this logic lives under surveillance: "What will they think?" "Is this weird?" "How will they react?" These questions aren't about truth or meaning—they're about meeting expectations.

In a society where approval is the main currency, overt punishments aren't needed. Control becomes internal. People self-correct, censor, and limit themselves to avoid being "inconvenient" or "out of place." In anxious conditions, this is especially effective: people choose adaptation just to feel they belong. The system governs not through force but through voluntary self-abandonment.

The mechanism works because it's disguised as kindness. No one says outright what you must do, but you feel the stare, notice the silence, catch the shift in tone. Approval vanishes, and with it, your sense of stability. Behavior not validated by the system feels dubious—not because it's wrong, but because it wasn't recognized.

This breeds the ultimate fear: rejection. The system controls not just behavior but self-perception. If your sense of self depends on acceptance, if you lack an internal compass, you're forced to play. Being "good" becomes not a choice but a necessity, even if it feels wrong inside. Even if you see the falsity, you keep going—without approval, your reality feels unconfirmed.

Freedom begins with refusing to see approval as truth. It can be nice, but it's not a requirement. You don't have to be "good." You have the right to be real. If someone can only be close when you meet their expectations, that's not intimacy—it's a contract. You have the right not to sign it, no explanations or justifications needed, because your existence doesn't require permission.

Everything Is Pointless

February 13, 2012
Location: BsAs

Tons of people keep trying to force themselves to exercise. Someone buys an expensive gym membership, goes three times, then quits. Or they get a stationary bike for home, muster a week of willpower to pedal that dumb thing pointlessly, and soon it's just a clothes rack.

Or someone decides to go on a diet. Finds some "smart" book about proper eating. Cuts out everything tasty. Suffers for a couple of weeks, then inevitably finds an urgent, earth-shattering reason to devour half a cake.

And there they sit, drowning in guilt, feeling like spineless shit, ashamed of themselves. "What a weakling I am, no willpower, no motivation."

The supposed motivation for all this is usually one thing: wanting to please others. But that's not motivation—it's crap. Because, first, you can't please everyone, and second, why the hell would you even bother? And those who deep down believe they're worthless know that even if they sculpt a perfect body through superhuman effort, they'll still feel worthless inside. No amount of envious-admiring glances will change that.

Another motivation is this mythical "health." Like, "I'll be strong and skinny, totally healthy." So they gleefully wreck their joints jogging, strain their guts in the gym, and starve their body of carbs because some book says carbs are evil.

But nothing works. You can't fool yourself. It's all pointless, and it's obvious. "Oh no, I want to be beautiful to like myself"—bullshit. All this self-torture is just for others' approval. And it's never 100% (people will always find flaws), nor can it shift the deep-seated self-perception that led to this auto-torture in the first place.

I'm not even talking about how most people's daily activities—sitting on their ass in an office, then sitting on their ass at home—require zero physical fitness (in fact, the softer the ass, the comfier the seat). So there's no real need for this self-inflicted misery.

To me, the core problem is when a person's spark goes out. Instead of living, they just drag their burden, slogging through a forced existence, though honestly, they'd rather shoot themselves. Because there's no meaning. Tomorrow will be the same damn day. I earn money, I try to be good, I want a new car, I need to pay rent. On weekends, I'll hit a restaurant, after work I always watch TV, I want the best dish soap, and for vacation, I'll go to Mexico—but first, I'll buy a $2,000 camera and some lenses to post stunning pics on my blog so everyone sees what a talented photographer I am. Look, my fancy hotel, those cacti I ate, those fajitas. I so want you to envy me.

But why any of it? Mexico, photos, fajitas, new car, Saturday dinners, laundry detergent with a new improved flavor? We're improving our quality of life, we love comfort, good food, sex, we want to reproduce and give our kids a good education. And a big apartment with a plasma TV across from the couch to better park our asses. Because there's nothing else.

But one TV-watcher dreamed of being a firefighter (and was told it's nonsense), another wanted to be a singer (but was told it won't pay), aspiring artists and poets got the same verdict, actresses and dancers were mocked ("you, a clumsy cow?"), pilots and astronauts got theirs too. Stop dreaming, come back to earth, be an economist. Be a lawyer, an accountant, an engineer. You need to make money, you'll have a family to feed. To feed them, you'll need to start one. Settle down, get married, it's time for kids, come on, live by the rules, don't act out.

Who needs your spark? Who cares about your dreams? There's no word for "want," only "must," and dreams must be forgotten because there's only duty. Who you'd be if you were yourself doesn't matter to anyone. Then you wouldn't need gyms or diets—you wouldn't be so listless and miserable, feeling time slip by while life passes you by, not even knowing who you are. A person walking their own path doesn't just walk—they run, losing their shoes, toward what they really want. They're curious, impatient, alive, burning—how would they even get fat?

All that fat on your body is fat in your brain, fat encasing your true essence, which you were once forbidden to know. Which was "nonsense," "won't make money," "where do you think you're going, idiot," "stop daydreaming, dumbass, do your homework." That fat is a dead dream, and the listlessness is from living someone else's life. Then smart people come along, babbling about "motivation." Shitty word, invented by those who need you to live by others' ideas. Hammer them into your head and convince yourself they're your own values. You must want, and if you don't want to want, we'll make you want to want.

And there's no universal way to wake up.

***

(Spoiler: there is, it's in the book *Cordyceps: The Neural Network That Controls You*, Marina Karlova, 2025)

Politeness as Self-Suppression

Politeness isn't a neutral trait—it's a built-in filter through which the system regulates behavior without overt violence. Being polite, in the systemic sense, means suppressing anything that might disrupt social smoothness: irritation, fatigue, disagreement, rudeness, emotion, directness. This isn't about interactional culture—it's about systemically stifling the living.

Politeness becomes a behavioral model where you don't just filter speech—you filter yourself. You're trained to suppress your first reaction, bury anything inconvenient, and say not what you feel but what's acceptable. Over time, you stop distinguishing where reality ends and the script begins. You say "everything's fine" when it's collapsing. You say "no big deal" when you've just been humiliated. You say "I'm okay" when you're in pain. Because otherwise, you're impolite. And impoliteness threatens the social body.

This creates internal discipline: you monitor, regulate, and punish yourself. You become the overseer of your own expression. Every emotion passes an internal filter: Is it permissible? Will it disrupt the vibe? Will it be seen as hysteria, weakness, or pressure? If the risk of deviation is too high, the emotion is cut off. The body remains, but the feeling is bracketed out.

The result is a permanent role. People live not as subjects but as actors. One facade at work, another at the store, a third at home. The more "polite" someone is, the more masks they wear. They can be courteous, pleasant, correct—yet completely detached from their sensations. They don't conflict because they don't know what they want. They don't argue because they lack grounding. They don't step out of bounds because they've forgotten where those bounds were before they became habit.

Rejecting politeness in this sense isn't rejecting respect—it's rejecting substitution. Respect is a dialogue with another while preserving yourself. Systemic politeness is abandoning yourself for approval. True freedom begins where you stop being polite at your own expense—not because you're aggressive, but because you're alive.

Self-Esteem as an Internal Overseer

Self-esteem is one of the system's slickest tricks. At first glance, it feels like an internal gauge: how you view or value yourself. But dig into its structure, and it's clear: self-esteem isn't about you. It's a reflection of an external scale, embedded through repetition. It's not self-judgment—it's a copy of someone else's gaze, hardwired inside.

From childhood, you're told to have "healthy self-esteem"—neither too low nor too high. In other words, one that doesn't bother others, doesn't irritate, doesn't seem suspicious. Essentially, it's about forming an internal filter to judge your behavior, appearance, thoughts, and ambitions through the eyes of a hypothetical observer.

Self-esteem isn't a feeling—it's a control mechanism. When you think, "What if I look stupid?" "Did I overdo it?" "What will they think?"—that's not you. It's the embedded observer, activated by the system. You no longer need an external censor—you carry it. You check yourself against an invisible norm: Am I adequate, likable, appropriate, professional? Any deviation sparks anxiety: "Something's wrong with me," "I have self-esteem issues."

But these issues aren't personal—they're a symptom of being raised in a logic where your worth was always tied to someone's reaction. First parents, then teachers, then the collective. You weren't taught to be yourself—you were taught to conform. Even "confidence" in this framework isn't inner strength but the ability to make the right impression. That's not freedom—it's successful adaptation.

The system doesn't want you to move beyond self-esteem, because beyond it isn't chaos, as it claims, but freedom. Without the scale, you're ungovernable. You don't rely on praise, don't need approval, don't fear looking "wrong." You stop playing "adequate person" and start navigating by meaning, not reaction. That's the real threat to the system.

True self-respect starts not with proper self-esteem but with rejecting the idea that you need to be evaluated at all. Not because you meet standards, but because you exist. Self-esteem is always a reaction to a scale. Freedom is refusing to acknowledge its authority.

Creativity in the Bathroom
September 21, 2008

Sometimes creativity fails simply because we can't let ourselves sing in the shower.

Some might relate: you're splashing in the shower, in a great mood, dying to sing—the acoustics are perfect, your mouth's free, but you stay silent.

Because, damn it, you know the neighbors will hear—those acoustics work both ways. And what will they think? Maybe your song choice is lame. Maybe your voice will sound awful. Maybe you'll hit a wrong note, and then how do you face them in the hallway, God forbid? The whole scenario is so horrifying, it's easier to skip the joy altogether.

The shower example is small potatoes. It's your home, and honestly, neighbors would probably be the ones embarrassed for judging your singing if you bumped into them. People sing on the street—usually far from home, at night, and very drunk—and you react in a predictable way. :) Because in that moment, you're society, the neighbors, the judge. But they don't care about you. Their singing isn't exactly melodic, but the "performers" are passionate. It's not commercial creativity: they're not solving a task, their minds are too sloshed for that, but they're connected.

That's why artificial highs don't help designers: fear shuts off, but so does reason. It might work for artists, but it's too costly in every sense. We once spat venom at each other here, debating whether designers need to draw by hand. That's a fight about externals, skills. If we ditch the truth that nobody owes anyone anything, it's better for a designer to first try being an artist, in the broadest sense. It's self-expression without fear of judgment. To unfold, you need to step out of the narrow corridor and see your real possibilities. Sing, dance, carve wood, embroider bunnies—whatever, but do it without looking back, without evaluation, without comparison.

When you can sing in the shower, ignoring neighbors, silencing the inner judge, not evaluating, not even slightly wanting to look better than you are, something shifts. Some sing in the shower shamelessly, but often it's because they know they're good, so those damn neighbors can shut up and listen to how awesome it is. That's the flip side of the same coin: you can flaunt your skill all you want, but there's nothing behind it.

So, letting yourself sing through yourself, not thinking about quality or neighbors, is hard even alone, in your own bathroom, physically naked.

***

Are You Good?

You've been trained to be good. Not alive, not honest, not feeling—but good. Convenient, polite, predictable, non-threatening. You've learned to suppress impulses, filter words, soften reactions, guess what's expected. Not because you're weak, but because in this system, that's how everyone else survived. You've learned to monitor yourself: how you look, how you sound, how "appropriate" you are. You've internalized an overseer that asks: "Is this okay?" "Am I too much?" "What will they think?" This overseer speaks for "everyone"—parents, teachers, bosses, partners, random strangers. It says: "Be adequate," "Don't overdo it," "Don't ruin the vibe." And you comply because you want to be accepted.

But here's the question: Accepted by whom? Approved by whom? Who exactly do you want to validate you? And why is their opinion worth more than your life? Why do you let external reactions rewrite your internal reality?

You're good. But for whom?

Until you ask this question, you're trapped. As long as you strive to be "correct," you're not free. Because real freedom doesn't start with approval—it starts when you stop waiting for it.

What I Wanted to Say When I Was Little
October 11, 2008

That famous poem—"What Is Good and What Is Bad?" by Vladimir Mayakovsky—always struck me as one of the most depraved things in the universe...

Tiny toddler told his Dad:
"I am puzzled so!
What is good and what is bad?
Answer if you know!"

Secrets I will always shun —
Nothing could be worse!
All that Papa told his son
I have put in verse.

If the wind tears down the roofs,
If the heavens spout,
That is bad — why, even goofs
Will not venture out.

Sun has conquered rain and cold,
Sun shines over all —
That is good for young and old,
Good for big and small.

If the boy is black as pitch,
If his face has dirt on,
Then his skin is bound to itch —
And that is bad for certain.

If the boy likes soap and water,
Toothpaste, brush and comb,
Then he's very good and ought to
Be a pet at home.

Some boys bully, bite and hit
Boys but half their size.
Boys like this I can't permit
Verse to advertise.

Other boys will never strike
Smaller boys. That's good!
Boys like this we're bound to like —
That is understood.

If the boy destroys and tears
Picture books and toys,
Each October-child declares:
"What a bad, bad boy!"

If his eyes to books are glued,
If he's never shirking,
Then the boy is very good,
For he's fond of working.

This boy met a crow and scampered
In a dreadful funk.
Coward! He is sorely hampered
Through his lack of spunk.

Others would not be afraid to
Tackle birds of prey.
Good! Such spunk's a mighty aid to
Boys on life's long way.

Some boys' shirts are black as ovens,
Yet the boys seem glad.
People call them dirty slovens.
Don't you think they're bad?

This boy's shoes are always shiny
Just as shoes should be.

Though the boy is very tiny,
He is good, you see.

All must grow from small to big —
Nothing ought to balk us.
Boys are bound to grow up pigs
If the boys are porkers.

Tiny toddler understood.
Tiny told his dad:
"I will always do what's good,
Never what is bad."

It's a vile fucking manual for turning a child into a socially useful robot. A guide to slapping labels on everything. Any clear-thinking kid would see it's one of the nastiest poems out there. All it teaches is that doing what you want gets you labeled "bad," but following society's orders earns you "good." Maybe Mayakovsky meant something else, maybe he was mocking this idiotic classification of kids. But it's marketed as a children's poem. Kids take it literally.

Be convenient for society, school, parents, act properly—and you'll be called good. Explore, be yourself, break stereotypes, do what you love—and you'll be called bad.
Forget your desires, live an imposed life—you'll be good. Chase approval. Make it the goal of your meaningless life. Shame yourself, because deep down you know: if society saw the real you, it'd call you bad, and you'd have to live with that.
You, by yourself, are of no interest to anyone.

That's the shit we internalized well.

***

Who Are the Judges?

Self-esteem is when you judge yourself with someone else's voice. And the "judges" are those whose voices you first believed. They vary in form, but they're all parts of one system: the internal overseer watches from within, the external from without, but neither touches the real you.

One of the subtlest perceptual glitches happens when someone, used to being an object of judgment, automatically grants others the right to judge. They're primed to be dissected, measured for sanity, understood or misunderstood, approved or condemned. But they never ask: Who are these people? What's behind their perception? What guides them? Are they even a valid reference point?

The error isn't in caring about others' opinions—it's in treating those opinions as objective. When you see yourself as an object of judgment, you assume there's a subject out there—clear-sighted, sober, wise, knowledgeable. But the truth is, most "judges" are just carriers of templates. They're the ones who'll evaluate you because they've got a ready-made ruler to measure everyone by. A living person doesn't judge—they look, feel, listen, but don't slap on labels. They don't need to slice the world into categories.

This flips the whole coordinate system. Those who think mechanically wield power. Those capable of real perception stay silent. If you take the former's opinions as truth, you're not just wrong—you're handing your center to simulacra. You're trying to prove your worth to those who don't see worth at all. Not because they're evil, but because they live in the coordinates of norms, not life.

This glitch isn't personal weakness—it's the system's default setting. From childhood, you're taught to seek approval—in school, family, society—and you learn about yourself not directly but through the warped mirrors of others' reactions. Then you realize those mirrors are distorted. The ones whose opinions you took as truth are themselves living in fear, repetition, and rule-following. But because they've got confidence or just pushiness, you believed they knew better.

The way out isn't the "not giving a fuck about their opinions" but to see who is giving them. And recognize: if someone's judging, they're not seeing. They're not in contact—they're in a pattern. Their judgment can't be authoritative.
The truly alive don't judge—they resonate. If you're alive, you don't need external judges because you're no longer an object. And anyone trying to play judge reveals by that alone: they're long gone from themselves.

Reality by Instruction

The system pretends to describe the world, but it actually constructs it. Through language, norms, rules, and categories, it builds not a true picture but a map of permitted routes for thinking. The very act of thinking is pre-set: you're not asked to seek meaning but to choose from ready-made options—right or wrong, normal or deviant, success or failure, victory or defeat, good or evil. Anything that doesn't fit this binary grid vanishes as inadmissible, illegitimate, erroneous, or suspicious.

This model feels natural only because it's embedded in language itself. Linguistic structure revolves around oppositions: "if not A, then B." Doubting this logic is equated to weakness, hesitation is read as insecurity, and ambiguity is seen as a threat. From childhood, you're trained not to explore but to take a side. They don't ask what you think—they put you before a choice: with us or with them. "Who do you love more, mom or dad?" (This question baffled me as a kid because it's dumb, but "WTF?" wasn't an allowed answer.) This perceptual structure makes reality not alive, fluid, or unfolding, but frozen, like a table or manual. The world becomes a diagram, and you're a test-taker picking from a pre-set list.

This creates the effect of thinking by instruction. The system doesn't demand reflection—it demands correct answers. Don't reason, just pick what's deemed right. Even if the question is framed falsely and all options are manipulative, the goal is to fit the template. Binary thinking benefits those in control because it's easy to monitor and enforce. Someone trained to choose between two pre-set options can't imagine having their own.

This logic seeps into every sphere. Instead of self-understanding, you're told to decide if you're an introvert or extrovert. Instead of "how do you live?" you get "how successful are you?" Instead of "what do you feel?" you're asked if your reaction is adequate. Even pain must be classified: anxiety or depression? Even relationships need labels: healthy or toxic? Experiences aren't lived—they're coded. If what's happening to you doesn't fit a category, it's deemed invalid.
The system holds power not through bans but by limiting what's conceivable. Nothing needs to be forbidden if you can't imagine beyond the manual. If someone sees, feels, or thinks differently, they're labeled unstable, weird, or out of place. You're left with two choices: stay silent or mimic—play the system to stay in it.

Binarity isn't just cognitive simplification—it's a power structure embedded in thought. It turns reality into a black-and-white scheme, doubt into a symptom, complexity into a problem. The first step to freedom isn't choosing between "right" and "wrong" but rejecting those terms altogether. The world isn't binary. It doesn't fit an instruction.

Duality as an Artificial Construct

Duality often feels self-evident. It seems natural that there's good and evil, black and white, truth and lies, success and failure. We don't question where this structure of opposites comes from because it's woven into language, culture, school grades, everyday reactions. But duality isn't a natural law—it's a constructed model, implanted in consciousness to control choice.

The world we live in is far more complex than dichotomies. It's not split into two neat categories. Everything alive is multilayered, fluid, nonlinear. No person is "just good" or "just bad." No decision has two outcomes. No situation exists in two states. Yet we're taught to think in pairs: you're either right or wrong, sane or strange, "in flow" or "in decline." This logic chops off complexity and confines thinking to rigid frames.

Historically, duality didn't arise to reflect reality but to simplify and discipline. Religious systems leaned on it—good vs. sin, salvation vs. damnation. Moral codes, state institutions, and educational standards cemented it. Not because it captures truth, but because it's convenient: it enables judgment, division, punishment, normalization. With two poles, you can impose the need to choose the "right" one. If you don't choose, you're suspect. If you choose wrong, you're mistaken. Thus, duality itself becomes a control mechanism.

This model shapes language too. We struggle to express what doesn't fit oppositions. We're not used to describing complexity, contradiction, fluidity. Language is reduced to binary constructs, and in this impoverished space, the possibility of speaking about a third way vanishes. We lose the ability to notice nuance if culture doesn't represent it. If someone speaks from this "third state," they're misunderstood—classified as deviant or a threat.

Duality isn't just a way to describe the world—it's a way to strip you of alternatives. Under the guise of logic, you're handed a frame. Under the guise of choice, a script. If you play these opposites, you stay in the system because it pre-set your options. Escape begins with refusing to accept this frame as the only one. Rejecting duality isn't rejecting distinctions—it's rejecting the coercion to choose between two when reality is far bigger.

The Ontological Cage

One of the subtlest forms of systemic pressure is the demand to take a side. From childhood, you're taught that in any situation, you must decide who's right, who's wrong, whose side you're on, and how you feel about it. Failing to give a quick, clear answer is seen as weakness, indifference, or betrayal. The idea that you might have a complex, contradictory, or undefined stance isn't allowed. The world is split into camps, and if you haven't picked one, in the system's logic, you don't exist.

This forms the ontological cage: you're recognized as existing only insofar as you take a position. Refusing a position is seen as refusing identity. If you don't define yourself, you vanish from the system's coordinates. You become elusive, intangible, unclassifiable—and thus ungovernable. The system can't handle the undefined; it only sorts: black here, white there. If you're neither, it will push you out, force you to choose, or slap on a label.

This coercion to be someone, to pick a side, to claim allegiance, is the root of binary consciousness. The moment you accept these rules, you're part of the scheme. Even if you choose opposition, you're still inside, because the logic of opposition remains untouched. You keep existing in terms set from outside, obeying a structure you didn't choose.

Many forms of social and psychological violence start here—with extorting self-definition. You're demanded to say: Who are you? Whose side are you on? How do you identify—orientation, nation, politics, personality type? It can look like care, curiosity, or understanding, but it's always about classification. The classified are easier to control, while the unclassifiable are a glitch. Glitches are either fixed or isolated.

Escaping the ontological cage doesn't mean picking a new position—it means rejecting the structure of choice itself. You can exist without a label, without allegiance, without a role, without a side, and still not be indifferent, passive, or weak. It means existing outside the model where existence requires a position. It means being, not by instruction, but because you are. That's not a position. It's ontology.

"I Got Rid of My Ego. Now I'm Better Than Everyone!"

August 30, 2010
Location: Baños

Disclaimer: If anyone accidentally recognizes themselves in this post—please don't take offense. I can see myself here too, say, from two years ago (to those who got caught in the crossfire during that rough time, my sincere apologies. Thank you for bravely enduring my spectacular idiocy). I think this is just something that can happen, like how we all wet the bed as kids.

So, take an ordinary person. Totally normal, with a standard inferiority complex, tangled in their own life, exhausted from trying to prove to themselves and the world they're not a piece of shit. One fine day (or week, or month), they find something. A lifeline, a crutch, a theory that suddenly feels like "enlightenment." Something that seems to tie together all their scattered thoughts and guesses, answering every question—Osho, Castaneda, Zen, Taoism, EST, Kozlov, Zeland, Carnegie, The Secret, primal therapy, religion, vegetarianism, healthy living, PEAT, or just a conceptual misanthropy. Whatever. Stuff about the ego works especially well. Any source that explains how it functions makes our ordinary person believe they've cracked the code, gained secret knowledge about the vile nature of pathetic humans (which they, of course, are above and beyond). Now they can sit back and chuckle at everyone else's dumb sandbox games.

Instead of recognizing the "monster" and taming it, they go blind and soar to the heavens, propelled by an ego inflated to galactic proportions. They're thrilled with their unmatched awesomeness and irresistibly drawn to playing guru. A friend comes for advice? Wham!—a smack on the ass: "That's your ego! You're on the wrong path! Shut up, only I know the right way, you insect, you've got a long way to go. I'm done, stop wasting my precious time, you miserable wretch!" Satisfied with their advanced state, they go on jerking off to their supreme virtue and spiritual depth.

If that friend doesn't show up (it happens), our guru, unable to contain the proselytizing itch in their ass, goes public. Forums, social media, blogs, any place where people swap life experiences and problems. Plenty of room to shine there. The silly issues of "unconscious" idiots—our Person (capital P, obviously!) cracks them like nuts. Oh, that irresistible urge to enlighten the ignorant masses...

Sometimes they skip the public rants, which isn't necessarily better. Without public outbursts, all that "goodness" dumps on loved ones, and loved ones deserve better.
But those outbursts—public or private—are essential. Without them, there's no fuel. They're the hot air for their ego-balloon. The victims' reactions don't matter. They agree? Great! Share some books, then laugh together at the stupidity of the rest of humanity. They argue, get mad, try to hint the Person's off? Even better—they're just dumb, sleepy flies, how could their wooden brains grasp the rational, kind, eternal truth our Person is (out of pure altruistic nobility) trying to deliver? Their egos are totally unhealthy, bloated with pride, utterly unready to accept the goodness and light offered on a silver platter. Fucking morons!!!

What happens next?

Back to square one, but in worse shape. Self-deception never simplifies life. Sooner or later, the Person will likely realize they're still in the same shit, just spraying it with vanilla deodorant and covering it with pretty rugs for a while. And while they were at it, the pile grew, and now it's unclear where it's safe to step—under those rugs, you never know what's lurking. Here's where you've got to grit your teeth, toss those shitty rugs in the trash, and try to embrace what you find. Sometimes that "shit" is just a learned hallucination.

So, anyone got friends like this? :)

***

The Language of War in a Culture of Peace

A hallmark of the binary system is its tendency to frame any disagreement as conflict. Even if it's about opinions, experiences, or perceptions, the system demands you decide who's "right" and who's "wrong." The moment two viewpoints appear, binary thinking turns it into a showdown. You're either for or against. You can't just observe, reflect, or be in the process of understanding—because in a binary culture, that's seen as dodging, passivity, or weakness.
This creates a model of perpetual war. Even in peacetime, the language stays militaristic. We "defend our stance," "fight for truth," "debunk lies," "expose manipulations," "go on the offensive," "hold our ground," "launch an argumentative attack." A debate becomes a battle, an argument a weapon, disagreement a challenge, and neutrality a cause for suspicion—whose side are you on?

Binary logic leaves no room for real dialogue because it assumes one is right, the other wrong. This eliminates focused joint reflection, exploratory thinking, and seeing the other as a subject. Instead, it's a simplistic scheme: who wins, whose version is stronger, whose claim is more convincing. Even a peaceful talk becomes a battlefield, judged by argumentative strength, logical coherence, and the ability to "come out on top."

In a binary-infected culture, even supportive language turns into pressure. You must "stand by your people," "hold your position," "not back down," "be strong." Express doubt? That's betrayal. Change your view? That's weakness. Opt out of the fight? You're indifferent. This fosters constant polarization, making it harder to exist in silence, reflection, or genuine search.

This language is everywhere: public debates, social media, expert arguments, activism, even psychology. Therapy has become a space where you "work on yourself," "step out of your comfort zone," "overcome resistance," "fight your inner critic." Everything is framed as struggle, conquest, effort, tension. Thinking itself has become tense. Until this model is recognized as a structure, it keeps setting the tone.

Escape comes only by refusing to join the war. This isn't surrender, defeat, or agreement—it's rejecting the logic of warfare. Stop seeing reality as a field of wins and losses, and you reclaim the ability to see the other as other, not an enemy. Think not to win, but to understand. Only then can you notice complexity without reducing it to a scheme.

The Illusion of Choice: The Trolley Problem

The trolley problem is a famous philosophical thought experiment, often used to discuss moral dilemmas. On the surface, it's an ethical question: if a runaway trolley is about to crush five people, but you can flip a switch to divert it to kill one, what do you choose? But beneath the ethical veneer lies not a moral debate but a covert programming of thought. It's a simulation with a rigid binary structure where all answers are false, trapping thinking in an artificial corridor.

The person in this experiment is placed in conditions where the only choice is between two bad outcomes. No time, no alternatives, no chance to question, reflect, or step back. No option to say, "I'm not playing this game." The setup itself is violent—it doesn't allow escape, only participation. It's not a question of "what would you do?" but a demand: "you must choose." That's the crux. It's not about morality—it's about forcing you to pick within someone else's script.

The effect of such tasks isn't to help you understand yourself. Their function is to embed binary structure as "natural" in your mind. If you're repeatedly told that every choice involves sacrifice, loss, or tragedy, you start seeing reality as a web of inevitable dilemmas. You learn to function within violence. You stop looking for a third move. You no longer question who created the situation or why it's framed as choiceless. You just "accept the rules" and aim for the "least bad" option.

This is the system's logic: not to solve, but to narrow. Not to find a way out, but to maintain the illusion of choice within a pre-set grid. If you refuse to play, you're labeled a coward, heartless, or unworthy of dialogue. The right to step outside the model is revoked. You're not a subject—you're an executor in an ethical theater, proving you can make tough calls. But the choices were already made for you.

Paradoxically, the trolley problem's framing proves its structural violence: no one asks who built the tracks, why the train can't stop, where the brakes are, who put people on the path, or why your only options are to kill. Instead, you're given four letters—F, U, C and K—and told to spell "happiness." If you fail, they say it's your moral failing. In reality, it's the absurdity of the construct.

Exposing such tasks isn't about finding the "right" answer but seeing the mechanism. This isn't philosophy—it's a technique to implant binary thinking. Real life rarely has two inevitable outcomes. But if you're trained to think this way, you become someone who, stuck in the system, doesn't seek an exit—because you've been convinced there isn't one.

Chess as a Model of the System

Chess isn't just a game—it's a coded model of a world where every piece knows its place, every move follows rules, and the process hinges on inevitable conflict. It's not a training ground for abstract thinking but a textbook for embedding in a system with rigid hierarchy and binary logic.

No piece in chess steps beyond its function. A pawn can't become a queen unless it reaches the board's edge. A knight can't move forward. The king is central but restricted. The game's mechanics rest on distributed value and fixed roles. Possible actions are determined not by the situation but by pre-set status. Every element serves a function within someone else's architecture.

The board is split into black and white, victory comes only through total submission or destruction. Conflict isn't just built in—it's the game's essence. Any advance isn't an escape but a tightening of control. A draw is a script glitch, not an alternative. Even sacrificing a piece serves calculation, and defense is part of offensive logic. Everything submits to a game that never asks why it exists.
Chess isn't a space of freedom—it's a map of binary thinking. All roles are pre-known. The board is a simulation of a struc-

ture where every move reinforces the existing order. The game doesn't invite doubt—it demands optimization.

Thinking like chess means thinking in terms of efficiency within a pre-built model. Creativity is allowed only within functional bounds. Winning at chess isn't freedom—it's peak adaptation to the system.

When a child is taught chess, they're not offered logic development but order training. Logic is embedded in discipline. The ability to make moves is tied to silent consent. This isn't thinking's growth—it's its formatting. Chess isn't "bad"—it's a precise reflection of how the system teaches you to see the world: a field with no exit, only clear roles, scripts, and end goals. Even if you win, you're playing by rules you didn't choose.

The author, by the way, enjoys a game of chess. But absolutely refuses to live in one.

What Happens If You Don't Choose

When someone stops picking from pre-set options, the system glitches. It doesn't know how to handle someone who hasn't joined a camp, picked a side, or reacted as expected. They become an anomaly—unclassifiable, and thus unintegratable into the structure.

In a binary thinking culture, refusing to choose isn't seen as a conscious act but as weakness, immaturity, cowardice, or irresponsibility. The system reads this not as freedom but as a flaw. Its job is to eliminate ambiguity, push for a choice, force clarity, and declare "you can't do that." Demanding you "take a stand" or "clarify your position" isn't about honesty—it's about control. It's about keeping you in a known coordinate grid.

But what happens if you don't comply? If you don't debate on their terms or play a game with a pre-set meaning? The system loses power. Its control isn't based on force but on consent. You hand it power not when you lose, but when you agree to play by its rules.

Refusing to choose between poles isn't dodging responsibility—it's a new kind of thinking, the start of escaping alien logic. It's not passive but autonomous. You don't pick "for" or "against"—you exist outside that construct, not from detachment but from rejecting the frame. You stop seeing the system's language as the only way to describe the world.

This creates a third space. Not a compromise or middle ground, but a new dimension where polarity itself dissolves. Where "who's right?" becomes "why are we even asking this?" Instead of two options, a new coordinate emerges. This space defies schematization, which is why it escapes control. It doesn't need right answers—only the living process of thought, open to countless forms of perception.

Only here can you truly see. Not fight, not prove, not take sides, but observe and understand what lies behind the structure. While you're in the binary system, you're busy upholding its architecture. But step outside, and you see the world doesn't need division to make sense.

About Toothpaste

June 5, 2011
Location: BsAs
Music: Cloudy Day - J.J. Cale

I hate toothpaste caps that screw on instead of flip open, but you can never tell because those bastards don't put that info on the package, and the boxes aren't always openable-closeable. When I see a box sealed shut from all sides, and I'm not sure I remember which cap this brand has, I panic. But that's just poetic whining.

Then I made a shocking discovery. I gave in to my lazy nature and (horror!) left the toothpaste tube uncapped. Here's the revelation: nothing happened to the toothpaste. It didn't spill, dry out, disintegrate into atoms, or run off to commit mass murder. I checked—the next day, it was still calmly sitting in its tube, perfectly pasty.

So, this anecdotal cause of family fights over uncapped toothpaste tubes, per my discovery, is total, baseless, unscientific heresy with no logical grounding.
Guys, don't fall for the provocation. Let's wake up from this nightmare and feel how damn liberating it is to stop capping the toothpaste tube every time, to just leave it open. Hell, throw the cap out the window. Ladies, back off the guys and go make some food.

Update: I want to clarify about screw-on caps, in case anyone missed the depth of this issue. I don't get who the monster was that invented them. After squeezing paste onto your brush, you're in a total bind: one hand's got the tube, the other's got the brush with paste. There's no third hand to grab the cap and close the damn tube. So, you either put the brush on the sink (but the paste might fall off, meaning you start over; or if you stick it in a cup, the paste could drop if it's not firmly embedded in the bristles), or you set down the tube—but that's a losing game too, because an unsecured tube in a horizontal position requires ninja-level fine motor skills to cap, especially with a screw-on.

***

(Fourteen years later, the author acknowledges the sexist joke and admits it was idiotic.)

Suppression Through Communication

The system doesn't need overt violence if it can embed its structure into the fabric of communication. It doesn't matter where the conversation happens—at home, in a therapist's office, in social media comments, or at the family table. Communication becomes a tool of control not just when someone yells, but when language subtly serves the structure: smoothing, trimming, structuring the living into something predictable and acceptable.

Suppression happens not only through institutions but through speech. It's in conversation that the main field of manipulation, normalization, and subtle power-shifting unfolds. Instead of real dialogue—editing of reactions. Instead of acknowledging pain—rationalization. Instead of freedom of thought—"reasonable correction." All framed as "communication," but in essence, it's corrective intervention. With enough of these, you can no longer tell where you end and the program, operating through others, begins.

This section explores how language becomes the primary carrier of systemic suppression. We'll dissect not just how template-driven people speak, but how speech algorithms function, why they're used, and how to exit these interactions without internal distortion. Because if you don't see the structure, you start doubting yourself. But once you do—you're no longer part of the mechanism.

Recognizing Template-Driven People

The system isn't just upheld by power—it's sustained by transmission. Its primary code-carrier is the person infected by the structure, who's internalized it so deeply they retransmit it without realizing. They might be polite, caring, educated. But their language is the system's language. Their reactions, expectations, words—all betray them as conductors of the template.

Recognizing them starts not with their opinions but with a mismatch. You speak, but feel unheard. You share something alive, and get a scripted response: "you can't do that," "be wiser," "it's all in your head." The words seem normal, but their structure is dead. It doesn't resonate. You feel discomfort, like a thick glass wall separates your meaning from their reply. They don't argue or aggress—they're just not present. Instead of contact—a script. Instead of understanding—correction. Instead of dialogue—normalization.

This mismatch shows up in the body too. They may speak softly, but their voice carries tension. They smile, but their eyes stay cold. They say they want to "understand," but their posture signals rejection. In normal culture, these discrepancies are ignored. But in alive perception, they register instantly: the body doesn't match the words, the reaction doesn't fit the situation, the contact doesn't align with the stated intent. It feels like you're talking to a mannequin, not a person.

Template-driven people often use the same phrases, even if worded differently. "Don't worry," "it'll pass," "be simpler," "it's not that bad"—these aren't support, they're instructions. They're not said to hear you—they're said to mute you. They're not gestures of empathy but acts of normalization.

There's no interest in your essence, only a drive to pull you back into acceptable behavior. This speech doesn't come from an individual source—it comes from outside, as if you're hearing the system's voice through a human mouth.

Recognizing the template isn't about labeling—it's about orientation. Once you see the split between content and form, word and body, tone and meaning, you're no longer trapped. You stop expecting understanding where there's none, stop explaining yourself to someone who can't hear. You don't argue, prove, or justify—you exit the contact. Not out of spite or contempt, but for self-preservation.

The system reproduces itself not through rules but through carriers. If you learn to spot them, you stop being vulnerable. You're no longer fooled by appearances, you hear the split, and you recognize the structure—even when it smiles.

Speech Signatures of the System

The system rarely acts directly. It doesn't say "shut up"—it says "be simpler." It doesn't forbid—it "recommends." It doesn't devalue—it "cares." But language, like genetics, encodes everything. Those who transmit the system often betray themselves not by tone or intent, but by phrasing. These are the speech signatures of the structure: template constructs encoding suppression, normalization, control, guilt, detachment.

These phrases seem mundane, but their effect is always the same—cutting off contact. You share pain, and hear: "don't overthink it." You mention anxiety—they reply: "everyone lives like that." You admit it's tough—they suggest "go for a walk." None of these show an attempt to hear. They aim to close the topic. They may look like care, but they're always operations to suppress the signal.

Here are examples of such signatures:

— "You can't do that"
— "You're too sensitive"
— "You're overcomplicating things"
— "You should be grateful"
— "Everything happens for a reason"
— "You're not the only one"
— "At least you have..."
— "Be simpler"
— "Everyone lives like that"
— "You attracted this yourself"
— "It's your trauma talking"
— "That's just projection"

They share one trait: no interest. They don't want to understand or be with you—they want to normalize you. Framed as universal truths, they're actually bans on the living. Their "polite" and "kind" tone makes them seem harmless, which is what makes them so effective. You don't realize you've just been shut out of the dialogue.

These signatures aren't just words—they're algorithms embedded in everyday speech. Their goal is to seed doubt, shame, or self-censorship. They don't demand agreement—they demand subtle, invisible, voluntary submission. You're meant to convince yourself you're "overreacting," "inconvenient," or "wrong."

Recognizing these phrases isn't paranoia or aggression—it's discernment. If you hear one, freeze.

Don't respond immediately.
Hear the structure.

If you feel that familiar sting—"I'm not heard, I'm being folded, I'm ashamed"—chances are, you've just met not a person but a code. That's the moment to stop explaining and exit the contact—to preserve your connection to yourself.

System-Induced Stupidity

Stupidity isn't a lack of intelligence—it's a lack of freedom. It doesn't stem from weak cognitive abilities or poor education but from a structural glitch where thinking is replaced by retransmission. It's not a personal trait but a systemic effect. A person ceases to be an observing subject because their consciousness is fitted with a filter that only passes what the system pre-approves.

You can know languages, hold degrees, quote Kant—and still be stupid. Stupidity isn't measured by the volume of memorized information. It shows in the inability to see beyond the frame. Stupidity isn't just foolishness—it's the absence of access to alternative fields. It's thought that doesn't think because it operates within the permissible. In this sense, "stupid" isn't an insult but a technical description of a state where someone reproduces a template without tools to analyze it.

The system cultivates stupidity because live thinking threatens its stability. A live mind questions, exposes contradictions, dismantles certainties. Stupidity is safe: it repeats, justifies, defends. It can be polite, confident, even charming, but it doesn't see—and doesn't want to. Because seeing means stepping beyond, and stepping beyond brings anxiety. Anxiety is a sign of aliveness, which the system seeks to minimize.

In conditions where thinking isn't suppressed, stupidity is impossible. A mind unsevered from intuition and meaning unfolds naturally. Stupidity emerges where reaction precedes thought, where "why?" is replaced by "that's how it's done."

It's not a glitch but an outcome—bred by upbringing, normalization, and relentless repetition that trains you not to notice what's being repeated.

Thus, stupidity isn't a personal flaw but a sign of deep adaptation. People fully embedded in the system don't see absurdities because their filters block inconsistencies. If someone can't grasp the obvious, it's not because they're weak or lazy —it's because their aliveness was deactivated. They were taught to ignore signals, disable doubt, and take an imposed construct as reality.

Stupidity is dangerous not just as an effect but as a carrier. The system normalizes it not out of love for stupidity but because it needs a stable circuit where thinking doesn't arise. Once stupidity becomes habitual, it acts as an active filter—not just ignoring meaning but suppressing it in others. A stupid person isn't just a victim but a retransmitter: they don't notice absurdity but actively defend it, as their identity is tied to the template. They don't just avoid questions—they neutralize those who ask. This is the real danger: stupidity becomes a self-reproducing structure where doubt has no place. The system is safe not because it's strong, but because it's served by an army unable to see it exists.

"Never underestimate the power of stupid people in large groups."
— George Carlin

The Live Voice vs. the Language of the Norm

There's a subtle trap when trying to distinguish systemic speech. If a phrase sounds judgmental, does that make it a template? If someone says "this is shit!"—aren't they judging too? Where's the line between a live reaction and the system's voice?

The key difference is the source. Systemic speech speaks for the structure. It doesn't express an internal reaction—it retransmits an external norm. "This is wrong" always refers to an invisible scale, a pre-set rule system. Even if said calmly, without aggression, it carries normalization. It's not a stance but an alignment. It doesn't reflect a personal view—it dictates how things should be, excluding what doesn't fit.

In contrast, live speech comes from a subject. "This is shit!" isn't a rule, instruction, or attempt to correct another. It's an emotionally charged but honest reaction to mismatch, falsity, pain, or absurdity. It doesn't impose a scale, demand behavioral change, or calibrate. It says: I see this, and it makes me sick. It's a statement, not a regulation. It's the direct voice of a living person, not a formula from an evaluation system.

Systemic speech almost always sounds "polite," wrapped in softness, care, or supposed universal truth. It's rarely direct, which is its strength—and its parasitism: it doesn't attack, it envelops. A live voice, even if harsh or profane, is transparent. You feel it's not from a structure but from pain, defiance, or honesty.
To discern, it's not just what's said but why and from where. Systemic speech aims to pull you back to the permissible. Live speech marks a boundary you won't yield. The first hides as universal; the second comes from the unique.

So, it doesn't matter if someone uses sharp words or speaks softly—what matters is whose speech it is. If it carries a live "I"—angry, tired, or furious—it's a person. If it says "be good, don't overdo it, don't feel too much," even kindly—it's the language of the norm. And it's always against you.

Exercise:

— *"The weather today is total shit!"*
— *"How can you talk like that? It's not nice!"*

Question: Who's the asshole here?

Manipulation as an Integral Part of the System

Manipulation isn't a random communication error or a character flaw—it's a mechanism of a global process. Its structure fully mirrors the architecture of systemic power, just on a mundane level. Where the state uses protocols, hierarchy, and suppression, a person uses emotional jabs, blame, and logic-blurring. But the goal is the same: shift the center, secure control, impose the only permissible frame.

The Hammurabi paradigm, as we've explored, assumes a strict role split: a subject of power and an object of submission. One interprets, the other must comply. One speaks for the norm, the other justifies their position. Manipulation replicates this exactly: in a conversation, someone takes the role of interpreter, setting accents and defining acceptable reactions, while the other is automatically positioned as deviant. They no longer speak—they explain. Their words aren't taken as a message but as a symptom.

This is why manipulation persists even among close or equal-status people. The system both parties are embedded in already contains vertical thinking. The culture of communication is built not on coordination but on normalization. Not on joint meaning-making but on regulating deviations. Manipulation is the interface of this logic in daily life.

When someone says, "You take everything personally," it's not just a phrase—it's a statement from a position of control. It doesn't seek understanding, clarify context, or explore reasons—it makes a verdict. It marks a deviation. It labels you as a norm-breaker, setting a boundary of power above you, even if temporary or unofficial, but fully functional.

Psychology, with its advice to "not take things personally" or "work through reactions," often upholds this architecture: responsibility for distortion is pushed downward. If you're vulnerable, you must fix yourself. If you feel pressure, you must learn not to react. Normalization trumps analysis, and "what happened?" becomes "why do you react like that?" This is the systemic model at work. The conversation isn't about truth but acceptability, not essence but form, not freedom but the standard.

Manipulation, in this sense, isn't "bad behavior"—it's an extension of a model where live consciousness is a deviation. Any reaction beyond the expected becomes grounds for correction. Thus, countering manipulation isn't about reacting or defending—it's about restoring structure: I speak, I state, I don't have to be convenient to be understood. I don't have to be calm to be heard. I don't have to be compliant to be real.

The Structure of Manipulation

Manipulation isn't a personality trait or a sign of malice—it's an architecture of interaction built on distortion. It can be conscious or unconscious, crude or delicate, but its essence remains: one consciousness alters another's state not through direct communication but through covert field-tuning.

The primary goal of manipulation isn't to convey information but to change behavior—not through argument or request, but by bypassing. Manipulation doesn't hit head-on; it grazes.

It creates tension, shifts focus, injects doubt, destabilizes, triggers guilt, anxiety, or awkwardness. It works not by persuasion but by eroding boundaries.

This is crucial because many imagine manipulators as narcissists, tyrants, or sociopaths. But manipulation is often soft, "well-intentioned." Parents manipulate children, therapists clients, friends friends, partners partners. Not because they're "bad," but because the system embeds control algorithms in language and thought. Being direct, clear, and honest is rare. Hints, passive aggression, and emotional traps are the norm.

Manipulation always uses distortion. Context shifts, focus is hijacked, logic fractures, emotions replace arguments. You're no longer discussing what you intended—you're defending, justifying, or doubting yourself. That's its job: not to convince but to destabilize. The less you notice, the deeper you're pulled into a script where the center of gravity has shifted.

Understanding manipulation means abandoning the illusion that it's about intent. Intent can be kind, but the structure toxic. When you respond not to tone but to construction, you see the architecture. Manipulation stops being "personal"—it's a marker of the environment. You no longer need to take offense or prove anything; you see they're not trying to hear you but to adjust you, not to understand but to tune you, not to engage but to fit you into a template. At that moment, you can exit the loop—because you no longer buy the form.

How to Counter Manipulation?

If manipulation is a structure, not a personal trait, countering it requires analyzing the architecture, not judging the person. Confronting a manipulator head-on rarely works because manipulation is designed to shift focus, distort context, and drag you into an emotional swamp where logic drowns. It's not an attack—it's a distortion of the environment, so the response must be cognitive, not emotional.

Manipulation starts not with blunt pressure but with subtle shifts. You might begin discussing something important and, within minutes, find yourself debating your guilt, ingratitude, or "oversensitivity." This isn't a quirk of the speaker but a hallmark of influence architecture embedded in everyday communication. Manipulation never acts directly—it works by displacing the center of gravity, creating a gap between topic and reaction, question and answer. It not only twists logic but subtly introduces hierarchy: one is "calm and rational," the other "emotional and irrational." One becomes the measure, the other the object of analysis. This imposes not just meaning but a power position.

The way out starts with holding your line—not arguing, proving, or explaining, but returning to your logical field where you can see the attempt to derail you. The key is not getting sucked into the emotional quicksand where arguments lose meaning and you become vulnerable. Manipulation thrives on blurring boundaries—evoking shame, offense, guilt, awkwardness, or doubt in your reality. Where you cease to be a subject, the structure gains control. The effort isn't about resisting the other but about holding yourself.

It looks like this:

— Person A: "The weather's awful today!"
— Person B: "You're always complaining."
— Person A: " 'Always' isn't true—yesterday's weather was fine by me."

Or:

— A: "I don't like singing karaoke."
— B: "You're always so different!"

— A: "Not true—I brush my teeth and use the toilet like everyone else."

— A: "This movie's total shit."
— B: "You're just an angry person."
— A: "I'm talking about the movie."

— A: "Today I just want to lie down."
— B: "You're doing nothing again."
— A: "Not true—I'm doing exactly what I want."

These aren't about the "right phrase" but the structure of response. Subjectivity is held not by words but by clarity of where you stand. You don't prove you're "not like that." You don't scrub off their labels. You don't save the conversation.

You just refuse to let them strip your right to a logical statement.

Manipulation loses its levers when you stop proving your innocence. It can only pull you in. When you stay on your level, avoiding the lower register, not drowning in explanations, you preserve your contour.

Main Weapons Against Manipulation

Manipulation doesn't work in a vacuum. Its effectiveness hinges on your loss of footing—failing to see the structure, losing your meaning, searching for where you "overstepped" or "erred." The primary anti-manipulation tools aren't behavioral—they're about preserving your consciousness's architecture.

Logic

Logic holds structure. Manipulation relies on distorting cause-and-effect, swapping theses, shifting emphasis. When you track sequence, question consistency, or check reasoning, you keep the structure intact. You're not arguing with the person—you're refusing their frame.

Meaning

This isn't about finding truth but distinguishing signal from noise. Manipulation loves contentless phrases: "you're always," "as usual," "here you go again." These carry no information—they create an emotional fog. If you stay in the field of meaning, not sinking into the fog, the attempt fails—it has nothing to latch onto.

Occam's Razor

Not just for assessing motives but for saving time. If a behavior or phrase functions as manipulation, you don't need ten alternate explanations. You don't have to find good in a distorted structure. Cognitive economy lets you spot suppression frames faster and avoid them.

Fact-Fixing

Staying in the present—not in personality debates, character analysis, or past dredging, but in the specifics of what's happening. "You didn't answer my question" isn't an accusation—it's structural anchoring. When structure holds, parasitic dynamics find no entry.

Right to Pause

Not distance but refusal to play in a distorted field. If logic is broken, meaning blurred, and the frame pre-set, continuing the talk means entering their system. A pause restores control, even if it's just silence.

Another method (when nothing else comes to mind) is answering a question with a question. This dismantles hidden assumptions. Manipulation often poses as self-evident: "You're dramatizing again." Asking, "What exactly do you mean by dramatizing?" isn't defense—it exposes the construct. It shifts from unprovable emotion to articulated meaning, where manipulation becomes visible.

These aren't about "power" or illusions of rightness—they make manipulation structurally impossible. Where logic holds, meaning persists, and position is fixed, there's no room for substitution. Without substitution, there's no manipulation—just a failed attempt without a stage.

Hacking Manipulation with Its Own Weapon: Hierarchy Inversion

One of the most effective ways to neutralize manipulation isn't just refusing its logic but flipping its structure. Since manipulation always implies a hidden hierarchy—one as subject, the other as object of interpretation—a powerful act of disruption is not defense but seizing the interpreter's position.

When someone "kindly explains" what you "misread," "overdid," or "really meant," they take the upper position: they're the "objective" arbiter, you're the field of analysis. This shift makes manipulation stable: you're no longer a dialogue partner but a figure to "correct." Even if you disagree, being "read" puts you on shaky ground.

But if, instead of justifying or defending, you calmly ironize how they've assumed the observer role, you swap frames. You become the interpreter, they the observed. You don't escalate to conflict—you reclaim subjectivity and reset roles.
This doesn't need to be a joke or sarcasm. A question about their behavior suffices: "What makes you think you can explain what I feel?" or "Do you often feel the need to re-educate people?" The hierarchy crumbles. The manipulator loses the stage—not just challenged but dismantled.

This isn't a universal template—it requires cognitive stability, precise timing, and mental freedom. But it underscores the core: manipulation is architecture. If you can rebuild the construct, you escape submission because you stop being an object in their narrative and become the author of your own. The system hates when the object speaks first.

The author once used this instinctively. Facing a manipulation attempt—"everyone's fine, you're just too sensitive"—I didn't justify, argue, or prove myself. I asked: "Is your knack for manipulation natural, or did you train for it?" Then, without waiting, added that with their intellect, those skills could be used for something productive. That was enough: the interaction stopped, the control attempt collapsed. The manipulator was pulled from their superior position and placed under observation. The inversion structure broke—they no longer controlled, they were interpreted. Manipulation doesn't work when its author becomes the object.

Reinforcing the Material

Manipulation doesn't just aim to change your opinion—it aims to lower your rank in communication. It's not a dialogue of equals but a hidden stage where one controls the frame, and the other must explain themselves. The key marker is how roles are distributed. Who sets the focus? Who speaks for reality, and who for the "problem"?

Manipulation doesn't always start with rudeness. Often, it begins with normalcy—a familiar phrase, an innocent clarification. But the result is a shift: you're no longer a subject but an object of observation. While you fight to be heard, you're already playing by their rules, cast as something to be decoded, adjusted, or doubted.

Breaking this stage isn't about fighting but refusing the role distribution. You don't need to justify—your words don't need rewriting. Meaning doesn't need to be "normal" to be valid. When you return to structure—meaning, logic, fixed context—manipulation's architecture loses grip. It thrives only where you stop being a subject.

Entertaining Philosophy

Most people don't read philosophy not because it's too complex, but because it's presented so drearily. Dry, detached, with academic bleaching of meaning. But strip away the husk of "authority" and "scholarship," and you see that real philosophers aren't saintly sages—they're people who smashed their heads against reality's wall harder than most. Their texts aren't instructions but letters from cages. Attempts to break free, explain, warn, or sometimes just howl.

This section isn't a textbook recap. It's a tour through those who, long before us, spotted the system. Who tried to crack it open with words before we had a theory of parasitic control. Each had their lens, their pain, their point of attack. Some struck at morality, others at power, others at language. But all, in their way, exposed the lies embedded in thought.

We won't quote fancy formulas. We'll pull from philosophy what's relevant today—in a world where power no longer wears crowns, and algorithms don't look like despots. Where control is mundane, division polite, and people don't even notice they're in a spectacle because they've forgotten the stage exists.
First up is Machiavelli, because he bluntly laid out how control works—no excuses, no humanistic gloss. Just as it is. Then come those who tried to hack the machine—or at least sketch its blueprint.

Machiavelli: A Manual for Aspiring Dictators

Machiavelli isn't compelling because he said harsh things or was a "cynical realist." He matters because he was the first to describe power as pure mechanics—stripped of religious pomp, moral garnish, or attempts to make it respectable. In The Prince, power appears as a system of managing perception, built on efficiency, calculation, and strategic control—not virtue, honesty, or justice.

He sees the prince as a figure needing not approval but control. To rule is to divide, pit interests against each other, keep tension between groups. Prevent unity. Keep them occupied with themselves. Create conditions where everyone's focused on their safety or gain, posing no threat to the structure. This isn't conspiracy—it's an engineering approach to system stability.

Machiavelli doesn't advocate fear for fun. He advocates risk minimization. If fear ensures more stability than love, the choice is clear. If seeming virtuous helps, fake it. If toughness works, use it. These aren't immoral—they're pre-moral. He describes not what should be but what is. And that's infuriating because it shatters illusions.

Crucially, Machiavelli doesn't invent the system—he documents an existing one. His book isn't just a "tyrant's bible" but a guide to navigating an already infected structure. He shows power isn't about lofty ideals but stable mechanisms. The core mechanism? Preventing unity. Where there's unity, there's resistance. Where everyone's divided, each is a predictable variable.

Division, competition, managed tension—these aren't side effects; they're the foundation. Machiavelli doesn't glorify this

—he just thinks playing otherwise is impossible. If his style repels you, that's fine. But to understand how the system sustains itself, he's essential. He doesn't justify power—he exposes it.

You can read him two ways. Some see a suppression instructor. Others, a cartographer of an infected landscape. If you study him to become like him, you're already a system agent. But if you want to spot traps and avoid them, he's an antidote. The system thrives not just on power but on naivety—on people not grasping the rules played against them.

In a reality infected by parasitic logic, Machiavelli can be not a domination manual but a survival map. He reveals the infected protocol's mechanics. Without understanding it, you're prey. His text isn't a license for cruelty but a diagram: how a structure functions where virtue is bait and compassion a weakness. This knowledge can serve not just to seize power but to shield against it.

And it's not just about states. This isn't only a dictator's guide—the same principles operate in office politics, school boards, relationships, therapy, Sunday calls with your mom. When someone divides, judges, or imposes, they're in the same scheme. No throne or crown, but the same mechanics.

Foucault: You're Your Own Buzzkill.

Michel Foucault isn't a philosopher you skim—not because he's complex but because he's too precise. He doesn't invite you to "see the world differently"—he insists your perception is already formatted. What you call "you" is shaped by the system, not mctaphorically but literally. You're classified, archived, fitted to a grid of norms, and plugged into a structure that produces subjects to template. This isn't a conspiracy—it's technology.

Foucault shows power isn't a guy with a club or a top-down decree. It's a distributed network embedded in language, norms, medicine, architecture, sexuality, notions of time and space. It doesn't need orders because it operates through knowledge's structure. You don't see pressure because it's the environment you exist in. You follow rules not from fear but because you don't notice they're there.

In Discipline and Punish, Foucault traces how external repression gave way to internal surveillance. The prison stopped being an exception—it became society's model. The panopticon, a circular jail with a central tower, isn't just architecture but a metaphor for power that's invisible yet omnipresent. You act "normal" because you know you might be watched. Even if no one's there, the mechanism works. Control is embedded in consciousness, and you become its carrier.

In History of Madness and History of Sexuality, he shows how science, medicine, and morality craft normative models, then fit people to them. First, a norm is built, then a deviation, then an institution to "correct" deviations. If you don't fit, it's not the norm's problem—it's yours. You become an object of treatment, education, or explanation, not a dialogue partner. Control isn't always forceful—it can be polite, therapeutic, even caring—but it's still control.

Read Foucault not to unmask another form of power but to deconstruct the idea of the norm. He shows "natural" is historically shaped, "objective" a result of interpretive battles. His philosophy isn't nostalgia for lost freedom but a challenge: to escape, you must know where the boundaries lie. They're usually in your head.

As long as you see yourself as "not fitting" and try to fix it, you're in the normalization architecture. Foucault reminds you: maybe you're not wrong. Maybe you just haven't seen where you end and the system begins. Once you spot that divide, the architecture wobbles. Its greatest feat isn't repression—it's getting you to police yourself. Voluntarily. The panopticon hasn't broken—it's just part of your internal interface.

Derrida: Smashing Binary Thinking

Jacques Derrida is the philosopher you either don't get or pretend to. He kicks down the door labeled "clarity" and dances on its splinters. But strip away the poststructuralist word-fireworks, and his point is clear: the core bug in thinking is binarity. Everything you know about the world is shelved into pairs: right/wrong, man/woman, body/mind, culture/nature, good/evil. These pairs are never equal—one always dominates. One's the norm, the other's the deviation. One's power, the other's submission.

Derrida calls this the "privileged position" structure. The first in the pair is the anchor. Male over female. Reason over body. West over East. The second is secondary, dependent, derivative. Even when you think you're judging fairly, you're in this construct. You're not choosing freely—you're picking from a pre-set menu. The trick? The structure feels natural but is constructed. And it reproduces power, even in language.

Derrida's weapon is deconstruction—not destruction, criticism, or mockery, but dissection. He takes a text, idea, or discourse and shows the contradiction, vulnerability, or parasite within its "stable" structure. He doesn't offer a new system or alternate truth—he says: look, your truth rests on assumptions you don't see. Spot them, and the structure loses absoluteness. It becomes an option, not a law.

Deconstruction isn't intellectual play—it's a way out of binary thinking where you must pick a side. While you argue who's right, you're in a system that divides. While you prove you're "not like them," you're embedded. If you're embedded, you're controllable.

Derrida doesn't offer a new truth but a way out of the logic where truth is something to find. Instead, he says: look at who set the question and why. This isn't metaphysics—it's political hygiene. Every time you accept an "A or B" choice as the only option, you feed a system that thrives on your consent. Hello, trolley problem.

His texts can feel like incantations. But wade through the fog, and he's saying one thing: if you're forced to choose, check who set the frame. And ask why you agreed.

Baudrillard: We've All Been Fucked, and We Didn't Notice

Jean Baudrillard isn't just a philosopher who noticed reality slipping away—he declared it's long gone. And no one cared because a simulation took its place, pretending to be real. Everyone just rolled with it.

Baudrillard introduces the simulacrum—a copy without an original. You're not looking at a thing but an image that once reflected something real, now just a shadow of itself. Ads don't sell products—they sell lifestyles, identities, vibes. Politics doesn't solve issues—it stages solutions. Sex becomes a performance. Revolutions turn into TV shows. Reality's archived, and a projection takes the stage, so convincing no one seeks the original.

A simulacrum isn't a lie—it's excess truth. So many layers of "meaning" pile up that the thing itself vanishes. TV doesn't reflect events—it produces them. Brands don't denote products—they create status. You're not just drinking coffee—you're in a narrative. This is hyperreality: the image outranks content, and signs become self-sufficient currency of meaning.

Baudrillard doesn't just critique consumption—he exposes the mechanism making it the social construct's core. People don't buy to own—they buy to affirm their place in the simulation, to feel they exist. In a world without anchors, only the interface remains. You are your appearance, your posts, your consumption. You are your avatar.

Global power here isn't dictatorship—it's spectacle. No need to repress—just broadcast. Instead of armies, mass media; instead of censorship, endless streams; instead of control, the illusion of choice. The more options, the harder to escape the simulation, because you're busy choosing between nonexistents.
Baudrillard pisses you off because he offers no hope—no barricades, just the claim: you live in a copy, love copies, and became a copy. To escape, you must admit you no longer know what's real. It's not pleasant, but it's honest.

Hatepost
May 7, 2009
Music: We've Got Tonight - Ronan Keating Feat. LuLu

I'm so fucking sick of cardboard tomatoes!!!

What the hell: cucumber, tomato—same tasteless crap, grass is grass.

"Big discovery," sure. But sometimes the bullshit in the world hits critical mass, and you get this sticky despair about the state of things. Fake beer, fake sour cream, artificial mayo, powdered milk, cardboard veggies, robot people...

And you're supposed to hustle to earn cash to keep buying this pseudo-food and pay for someone else's apartment. Is the tobacco in cigarettes even real, or is that fake too? :)

Oh, and sex without love. The "just sex" kind, where afterward you can't shake the feeling you just screwed yourself.

Stop the Earth, I'm getting off.

*****

Rousseau: You Were Fine Until They Raised You

Jean-Jacques Rousseau is often misquoted—romanticized as a "noble savage" fan, praised for loving nature, but his core point is missed: he was the fiercest Enlightenment thinker. Unlike his peers, he didn't seek to improve society—he questioned its foundation. Rousseau claims people aren't born corrupted—they become so when embedded in a system demanding adaptation and self-betrayal. Not because they're inherently wild, but because surviving in a world where being yourself means losing.

In The Social Contract, he drops a radical idea: sovereignty belongs to the people, not rulers. But he spots the catch—most can't express their will because they're trained to obey. Their "will" is pre-shaped by upbringing, religion, moral norms, and behavior codes. Rousseau first clearly shows control starts not with laws or violence but in childhood. When a kid is taught to be "good," "convenient," or "proper," they're prepped to be manageable.

In Emile, he offers an alternative—not utopia, but a demo of human growth without shame, coercion, or suppression of nature. It's not a naive forest fantasy—it's a political act against a culture turning people into functions. Rousseau believed someone detached from society doesn't worsen—they stop playing others' roles and become themselves.

His real radicalism isn't blaming power but indicting society's structure. He doesn't call tyranny evil—he says political hierarchy itself is a symptom of a prior catastrophe. Needing governance signals lost inner grounding. If you need an overseer, you don't trust yourself. And without self-trust, no matter the ruler, you're still subordinate.

Rousseau doesn't urge a cave return—he demands restoring the subject's original value before it's swapped for approval. His societal critique isn't anti-civilization but an exposé of its foundation: trading freedom for recognition. He's not a romantic but a surgeon, not offering dreams but amputating false premises. That's his true power.

Nietzsche: The Ultimate Morality Wrecker

Friedrich Nietzsche is both worshipped and feared—hailed as a visionary, damned as a cynic, quoted without grasp, often misunderstood. He didn't propose new morals, seek reforms, or aim to save humanity. He was about demolition. He didn't care for alternatives to the order—he wanted to torch its foundation.

Nietzsche was first to bluntly state: morality isn't truth—it's technology. Not divinely revealed or philosophically found—it's constructed for control. Good and evil aren't universal but labels slapped on behaviors based on their utility to the system. What makes you strong, free, independent is deemed evil. What makes you obedient, submissive, manageable is crowned virtuous.

This births what he calls slave morality: an inverted value system where the weak define "good" to neuter the strong. Christian ethics, compassion, humility, self-denial aren't humanistic—they're subtle submission tools. Instead of external violence, internal discipline. Instead of a tyrant, conscience. Instead of a whip, shame.

Nietzsche doesn't glorify strength as aggression—he states: to live is to want, act, be a cause, not an effect. His will to power isn't about dominating others but asserting your ability to be yourself without permission. It's independence from structures dictating who to be, how to think, what to shame, what to want.

His "death of God" isn't anti-religious propaganda—it's a fact: the old meaning-source lost force. No external sanction, no absolute guarantor. You're alone with yourself, emptiness, and the task to fill it. This isn't nihilism—it's a call for subjectivity. Meaning isn't found—it's made. Or not. Then you live someone else's.

Nietzsche isn't comforting philosophy. It makes old thinking impossible. He drives a wedge between you and your notions of good, truth, humanity. If it feels awkward, anxious, painful—good: you've spotted where the system lives in you and started thinking for yourself.

A side note: as radical as Nietzsche was, exposing morality and control, he was a victim of the system he critiqued. His misogyny isn't just "19th-century opinion" but proof of how deeply patriarchal programming runs. He dismantles morality yet reproduces its gender hierarchy. He's a genius—and an idiot. He didn't see in himself what he saw in others. The author condemns him for it. That's why he's here—not an idol, but a case study in missing the system within.

Sartre: Choose Yourself or Die

Jean-Paul Sartre rejected the idea that humans need external rules or divine manuals to make sense of existence. He obliterated the hope of a built-in life script, stating: there's no plan —not from God, society, or culture. All you're guaranteed at birth is freedom. No instructions, no success warranty, no right to whine about missing conditions.

His core idea—existence precedes essence—means you're born without a preset meaning, function, or identity. Everything you claim—job, beliefs, habits, gender, values—is shaped after you arrive, by you. You're not a template's product—you're a process of choice. Refusing to choose doesn't free you—it makes you material for someone else's project. Even passivity is a decision. Inaction is a volitional act. Freedom isn't a gift—it's a mandate you can't dodge.

Sartre's bad faith is when you hide behind a role, function, or excuse to avoid the anxiety of authoring your life. Saying "I'm just like that," "I was raised this way," or "things just happened" is a temporary dodge of subjectivity, donning a mask comfy for the world. But there's no life in that mask—no choice, no creation, no real action.

He doesn't call for heroism or romanticize autonomy—he leaves no escape. You are what you made of what was made of you. If you made nothing, it's not tragedy or sentence—it just means no one but you starts the process. Waiting for external meaning is a trap. Hoping for instructions is abdicating responsibility. Expecting someone to say how to be is not being.

Freedom terrifies because it's non-negotiable. You can't choose to be unfree—you can only pretend. If you still feel anxiety, if deciding without guarantees annoys you, if you sense no footing—that's good. It proves you're alive. Only the dead don't fear freedom—they've no choices left.

Heidegger: The Living vs. Consumerist Bullshit

Martin Heidegger is quoted less than people pretend to understand him. He wrote as if the world was built from untranslatable German constructs and humans from bewilderment. But strip away the Dasein and "thrownness," and his point is clear: he didn't aim to explain the world but to return humans to direct presence in it. He believed reality is lost not because it's hidden but because we stopped being with it—stopped being attuned, listening, perceiving.

Heidegger saw humans not as things, qualities, or subjects but as being-in-the-world. You don't "have" or "observe" the world—you exist in it as a mode of living. You're not a separate entity with opinions but part of a being-flow that shapes meaning's space. Your task isn't analysis or description but hearing what's already there—before concepts, schemas, tools.

He criticized technology not as machinery but as a thinking mode. Modern thought, per Heidegger, shreds being's fabric, turning everything into resources. Water becomes a hydropower plant, forests lumber, humans functional units. This shift kills not just poetic worldviews but the chance to be truly alive.

The issue isn't tech itself but its mindset: treating the world as an exploitable object. We stop being present. We stop hearing. We act by schema, embedding in constructs, forgetting that before schemas was simple, direct being. We live in forgetfulness of being, not noticing no one seeks it—just uses, formats, optimizes.

Heidegger's way out isn't archaic retreat or tool rejection but a shift in perception. Reality isn't a knowable object but a space of presence. Truth isn't correspondence but disclosure. Meaning isn't given—it arises in touching being, if you stop describing and start listening.

His philosophy isn't an action guide—it's a method to return to a state before you built a wall of language, diagrams, and goals between you and the world. You don't need to grasp him—just slow down. If you stop systematizing and interpreting, you notice you're in something always there, never named. That's being—not an abstract idea but what needs no explanation, because you're already in it.

They Were All Right

If we stuffed these philosophers in a room, they'd likely brawl: Machiavelli would call Rousseau a dangerous idealist, Derrida would gleefully shred Foucault's power apparatus into linguistic bits, Sartre would ditch the chat citing existential errands, and Nietzsche might storm out to avoid the human weakness fest. Yet, despite clashing styles, languages, and eras, they share a core: each tried to expose the structures of power, morality, language, and culture that cage humans and pass as reality. They distrusted the obvious, rejected the accepted, and probed weak spots in what most deemed unassailable.

Machiavelli showed power is engineering, not magic. Foucault proved control lives in details, needing no violence. Derrida exposed hierarchies baked into language's architecture. Baudrillard unmasked simulations replacing reality. Rousseau pinpointed when freedom becomes an external demand. Sartre erased excuses, insisting you are your choices. Nietzsche dared show morality can be a power technology posing as sanctity.

Different terms, contexts, pains—but one commonality: they saw "naturalness" as engineered. Rules aren't given—they're implanted. Norms are constructs. Language is the tool embedding structure. Unaware, you live in someone else's script, clueless it's not yours.

These aren't life coaches, mentors, or gurus—they're deconstructors. No need to trust them—read them as autopsies. They don't solve—they strip illusions. That's their strength. They're not the final word but the last to stand at the old paradigm's edge, seeing through it. Now, the talk shifts—to reality without facades, consciousness without scripts, a world beyond binarity. We leave them not because they erred but because they hit the limit. Time to move on. Welcome to a new ontology.

About Dreams, Goals, and Freedom

January 16, 2011
Location: Baños
Music: Mudhouse/Gypsy MC (Live From Amsterdam) - Jason Mraz

Once, an Argentine tourist, Rodri, walked me home. We had a slow, drunken chat.
"Kinda cool, your life," Rodri said, a bit envious. "Total freedom, doing what you want, living where you want. That's awesome."

"Here's the problem," I said. "As a kid, you dream of freedom, travel, whatever. It's safe because you know it's just dreams—impossible at 7 or 10. Where you gonna go from a sealed room with no doors? But when you get that freedom, you're unprepared. You can do anything, but you don't know what you really want. Dreams stop being dreams—since it's all possible, you gotta get up and do it. Unlimited choice paralyzes you. And experience shows fulfilled dreams rarely match the fantasy. Often, it's disappointment."

Lack of freedom stops you from thinking about what you truly want. In tight circumstances, you crave what's missing—working 9 to 5 makes you think sleeping in or free time equals happiness. In a grim Moscow winter in a tiny rented flat, a spacious tropical home seems like guaranteed bliss. Unable to travel, you imagine happiness in wandering the world with a backpack, no plans, no limits. Just examples. It's the old "grass is greener" trap—your neighbor's dessert looks tastier. After crossing rivers and snatching plates, you realize it's an illusion. Happiness, that bastard, still doesn't show, no matter what you do.

I had a goal: leave Russia, live where there's no winter. I did it. Now what? It was a distant, hazy dream. Its haziness meant I didn't think—what do I do when it's real? My other dreams were either done or dried up, so I arrived with an empty head. Buddhists might approve—freedom from desires is their jam. But for me, it turned into depression. I'm slowly realizing goals are necessary. Otherwise, head straight to a monastery and live quietly, because in the real world, no goals means no motivation, energy, or joy.

People say "just live" and be happy. I tried hard to get what's wrong with me, why I can't. They say a happy person can be happy anywhere, but I'm starting to think that's only possible with serious mental issues. Happiness is inside, they say, and you'll find it. Maybe, but that feels too detached from real life. It implies no goals—why do anything if you're already good? For me, no goals means no desire to live. Existential crisis, courtesy of such ideas.

Wanting to move to Argentina was great news—it gave me a goal. But I've no clue what I'll do when it's done. That's scary. I need longer-term goals. Otherwise, I'm haunted by the thought that there's no point living.

***

New Ontology

Meaning as the Vanished Variable

Meaning once stood at the heart of human existence—not as an abstract philosophical concept but as a living compass: why we live, what matters, what binds us to others, what gives weight to our actions. It was an internal foundation for choice, a guide for thought, a criterion for refusal. Meaning wasn't imposed—it grew from within, tied to the raw sensation of being alive.

But in modern culture, meaning has faded. Not banned outright, it was displaced.

First swapped for "goals," then "motivation," then "efficiency." People no longer ask what's meaningful—they're trained to be productive, adaptable, flexible, realistic. Instead of meaning, they're offered outcomes, achievements, engagement. Instead of reflection, evaluation. Instead of thought, functionality. This turns a living subject into a manageable, predictable, convenient unit.

Psychology, upbringing, education, work culture—all are rigged to replace meaning with external metrics. You're taught to conform, improve, overcome, strive for growth. But "better" here doesn't mean deeper or truer to yourself—it means closer to the norm, the permissible, the convenient. Meaning becomes surplus: it disrupts, slows, sparks questions, breaks predictability, pulls you from "resource mode" and "flow."

A modern person can live years in full external compliance—job, family, leisure, plans, goals, vacations—yet suddenly find an inner void. They do everything "right," as expected, but don't feel alive. They meet expectations but don't know why. They're within the norm but sense their absence in the construct. When they ask about meaning, they're fed more frameworks—self-esteem, motivation, boundaries—dragged back into a system where meaning isn't accounted for.

This erasure of meaning isn't a glitch—it's the system's design. A person seeking meaning is ungovernable. They might pause, refuse, question. They step beyond function, no longer a cog. That's why the system pivots to other questions: how to be effective, manage emotions, avoid burnout, stay "in tune." These aren't questions of a living mind—they're debugger queries for a program.

Returning to meaning starts with a raw truth: nothing you do matters unless it ties to your sense of reality—not to fitting in, duty, or normative expectations, but to what rings true. Meaning isn't a formula or slogan—it's a direction you feel. It's when what you do isn't alien to you. It's the experience that your actions carry weight, linking you to something larger than yourself. Everything else is just interface.

Living "Here and Now"?
February 14, 2011
Location: Baños

Can't do it. Yeeeep, read about it a million times, still can't wrap my head around it—how? If I'm living "there and later," how do I just switch to "here and now"? Do you smoke something for that?

A thought's brewing. I looked out the open window. Rain's falling, everything's wet, warm, smells of damp leaves and earth. I stand, watch, sniff, and like always in these moments, something inside aches, like some ancient thing, locked away for years, stirs. It's alive, damn it, and I'm terrified of it. If I let it out, who the hell knows what'll happen...

I wonder, maybe it's not just me with something locked up. Maybe we've all chained ourselves to hell long ago. The lock's huge, the key's lost, and opening it's scary. What if... something's in there?!
o_O

***

Cognitive Resonance

Cognitive resonance is a state psychology barely touches—it defies classification. It's not about balance, motivation, or "self-work." It's what happens when your inner sense and outer reality align. Not because you "think positive," but because you're no longer bound by a false structure. Your thoughts sound like you. Your actions match your feelings. It's not a norm or ideal—it's coherence between inner and outer, felt as truth.

In an adaptation-driven culture, cognitive resonance feels like a fluke. In truth, it's the natural state of a free mind. Most live in constant splintering—thinking one thing, saying another, feeling a third, doing a fourth, then wondering why anxiety creeps in. Their face doesn't match their tone. Words clash with gestures. The body says "no," the mouth "yes." The system calls this "adaptability," but it's a symptom of hacking—a sign of deep fracture.

Cognitive resonance starts when you stop performing. You don't apologize for reactions, justify choices, or explain your pain. This isn't aggression or narcissistic closure—it's acting from your identity's core, unpolished, unchecked against external views. You don't seek approval or need permission to be. You feel no inner distortion and recognize your return to self.

The system hates cognitive resonance—it's uncontrollable. Such a person needs no external validation, ignores shame tactics, sidesteps imposed explanatory models. Guilt can't manipulate them. They can't be sold "self-improvement." They're beyond explanations. They don't flee conflict but don't feed it. They stay on their frequency, not destroying others but not letting themselves be destroyed.

In resonance, there's no noise, no clash between knowing and speaking, feeling and acting. This person isn't idealized or always "calm"—they're present in themselves, undistorted. They're not "in resource"—they're in accord with themselves. This is the only alternative to the system's offerings. It doesn't fit algorithms, scale, or serve external structures. It either is or isn't.

If you read this and recognize it, you don't need confirmation. You know what's meant: this is you, no mediators, no interpretations.

Resonance Instead of Norm

"Norm" sounds neutral, even desirable. Normal means stable, safe, acceptable, clear. Being "in norm" means not standing out, not disturbing, not breaking predictability. Any deviation triggers reactions: anxiety, irritation, urges to fix or distance. This is how the system self-sustains—not through overt control but through standardization.

Look closely, and "norm" is no natural state—it's a conditional template. Derived from observations, averaged, fixed, then crowned as ideal. Norm isn't what's alive but what's statistically useful. It's a compromise passed off as essence. The dan-

ger? The normalization mechanism stays invisible, working not as command but as obviousness: "that's how it's done," "it's needed," "everyone does it."
Resonance, by contrast, isn't a template, rule, or normative trait. It's a phenomenon unmeasurable by rulers or checklists. The system rejects resonance—it can't be certified, standardized, monetized, or verified by tables. A resonant person is unpredictable, ungovernable, with their own compass, needing no permission to feel alive.

A norm-driven person constantly checks external markers: am I crossing boundaries, looking odd, speaking too loud, staying too quiet? A resonant person skips these. They don't aim for flawlessness or ideality. They're in a state of wholeness—not as a trait list but as the absence of inner conflict between who they are and how they act. This isn't about normativity—it's about truth.
Resonance isn't a category or trait—it's a way of being. You can't explain it, only feel it. In this state, external labels lose weight. You're on a frequency where "norm" zeros out. Where the living sounds, templates aren't needed.

A Long Post About the Crushed and Forgotten Desire to Draw

July 15, 2010
Location: Manta

Is there something you loved doing as a kid but dropped under pressure from circumstances/parents/school/society/etc.? Tried picking it up again? What happened?

Here's my example. I loved drawing since I could hold a pencil, and I was pretty good for my age, judging by memories. I did it constantly—home, kindergarten, then school... until sixth grade. Then I quit.

In school, I drew during lessons. My notebooks were anorexic from torn-out pages. When I ran out, I drew on anything—once, on school desks when paper was scarce (parents had to repaint that sad furniture). Teachers nagged me, scribbling diary complaints about "drawing in class!!!" like it was a crime. As if I drew with my ears and couldn't listen to their dull textbook drones. Funnily, those same teachers begged me to "decorate the door" for holidays (old tradition, maybe gone now). I'd obediently whip up festive posters on huge sheets.

Home wasn't thrilled either—I burned through paper tons, skipped homework, ignored chores, and ditched piano assignments. "Gifted" classmates (every class has them) backed the teachers, branding me the "crazy artist" obsessed with animal sketches. Leaving stuff on my desk during breaks was a mistake—things got stolen, crumpled, mocked, tossed around with jeers.

One screw-up crushed me. I left a nearly done drawing—two horses, my favorite theme—on my desk. Took me two days, loved how it was turning out. Came back to find someone had added falling poop under their tails. I can't describe the feeling now. It was monstrous. I didn't care that "they're just kids" (12-13 years old), that it was "just a joke," or that I could draw a thousand more. After that, I stopped drawing.

Tried picking it up—grabbed paper, sometimes something came out, but without practice, it fades. I'm scared of paper, maybe. I'll sit with a sheet and pencil for half an hour and draw nothing. My mind nags: "What was cool at 12 doesn't cut it now." I don't know what to draw, scared to waste paper (though with calligraphy, I don't care about felled forests). Talent needs nurturing—maybe mine wasn't great, but it was there—and I lost 15+ years. Those taunts, parent complaints, and the idea that drawing's "useless" or "harmful" still haunt me.

This sounds like whining, blaming others for my failure. Partly true. I'm not fishing for pity—those events are long gone. I just want to fix it and draw again. I think I know how. All these years, that abandoned hobby nagged me. I've hoarded paper, paints, pencils, markers, ink, pastels, art supplies—most unused, because I didn't think I could make anything worthwhile, and wasting stuff on crap felt wrong. I shunned fine art, except commercial design (totally different). I dodged paintings, graphics, galleries, snarling I don't get "high art."

No peace until I sort this out. :) I'm slowly starting again—timidly, on tiny sticky notes, because big sheets still scare me. I've got a brutal plan: buy a big, nice sketchbook and ruin it on purpose. In the nastiest, most unworthy way.

***

Wholeness as Rejection of the Implanted

The concept of wholeness in modern culture is often sold as a glowing restoration point—like you must "rebuild your wholeness," "piece yourself back together," or "return to yourself." This narrative sounds uplifting but stays trapped in therapeutic logic: you were "broken" and now need "fixing." It preserves the assumption that something was inherently wrong with you.

True wholeness isn't the result of repair—it's a process of purging what's been implanted. You weren't shattered; you were embedded in an alien structure. You were taught to feel shame, doubt, conform, strive to be "convenient." You took on rules, emotions, and self-perceptions that had nothing to do with you. You tried to be "normal" because otherwise, you'd lose access to love, safety, recognition.

Wholeness begins not when you feel "good" but when you stop sustaining what was injected. When you see that the fear of "being wrong" isn't yours. That shame isn't from your actions but from systemic programming. That the inner critic isn't conscience but parental training's echo. That anxiety isn't a flaw but a trace of unacknowledged pressure. This doesn't need "working through"—it needs deleting foreign code.

You don't need to fix yourself because you were never broken. You were captured by a system that convinced you otherwise. The idea that "something's wrong with you" is the core implant. It forces you to seek help, adapt, explain, justify. While you buy it, you're stuck in the construct. Stop believing it, and the exit begins.

Wholeness isn't completion or a static state. It's not an ideal but inner consistency—alignment between what you feel and what you allow in yourself, between inner impulse and outer action, free of imposed conflict wired into your thinking through others' words, fears, roles. Wholeness doesn't mean constant calm or total satisfaction—it means you stop violating yourself to conform.

True wholeness needs no explanation. It doesn't require display or depend on approval. You recognize it by the fading of inner tension, the waning need for self-control, the shedding of the urge to prove why you act as you do. This is freedom: not in conforming but in living without checking someone else's map.

Knowledge Without Judgment

The system doesn't teach thinking—it teaches judging. From childhood, we're trained that knowledge is about correct answers. Thinking is a path to a scorable, applicable formulation. Education is built on binary logic: answers are right or wrong; positions are justified or flawed. Even "creative" fields hinge on criteria, verifiability, alignment with external standards.

The result isn't developed thought but a trained reaction system. You evaluate, sort, classify, compare, but lose sight of your own understanding process. Knowledge becomes functional: it either yields results or it doesn't. Thoughts are "useful" or "harmful," conclusions "mature" or "infantile," reactions "adequate" or "unacceptable." Thinking itself bows to judgment, not exploration.

This kills true cognition. Real knowledge starts not with classification but with presence—observation, feeling, understanding without labels. When you think without instant verdicts, space opens for nuance. You stop chasing what's right and start seeing what is. This isn't relativism or logic's abandonment—it's a shift from judgment to investigation, from answers to observation, from verdicts to structural understanding.

The world is complex. Reducing it to "right/wrong" loses its essence. But the system thrives on simplification, rejecting thought that can't be tested. A person thinking outside the schema becomes "unclear," "inconvenient," "difficult"—unscorable, unembeddable. So they often silence themselves or translate their thoughts into checkable formats.

The way out starts with firing the inner examiner. Recognize that a thought's value lies not in provability but in opening new dimensions. Understanding can be real without instant formulation. Observation itself is an act of knowing. When you return to non-judgmental thinking, you stop being the system's object. You become a subject of cognition again.

Knowledge without judgment isn't chaos—it's trust in your perception. It's tolerance for uncertainty, attention to context, holding contradictions. The system doesn't teach this. But it's the only thinking that's still alive.

Who Am I If It's All a Matrix?

If the world is a system—standardized, normalized, ruled by control logic—a natural, perhaps inevitable question arises: who am I if everything offered isn't mine? If the language I think in was implanted? If my reactions were shaped by environmental pressure? If desires, goals, values were stitched in by culture, upbringing, ads, and fear of nonconformity? What's left if you strip it all away—and is anything left?

Here, psychology ends, and ontology begins. The question isn't how to "improve," "rebuild your personality," or "find what I want"—it's who's asking. Who says "I"? What's the center sparking reflection, perception, observation? This isn't about self-esteem or inner parts—it transcends the "mind as construct" model. It's not personal—it's structural. Not psychological—it's ontological.

Purge the implanted code, and you don't find emptiness—you find essence. Not a "personality" with traits but an aware field where experience arises. It's not static, not will-driven, not structurally fixed. It's not a "decision hub"—it's perception without filters. Normally, you're fused with imposed masks, but strip them away, and there's no void—observation persists. You're still here, just without the interface.

This sparks a new ontology. The old one rested on duality: subject vs. object, norm vs. deviation, truth vs. error. Its logic was binary. But if observation exists beyond implanted language and defies these frames, being's structure stops being linear. What seemed hierarchical unfolds as a network. What looked like a ladder becomes a fractal.

A fractal model of being isn't esoteric fluff or poetic imagery—it's a precise description of a structure where each part mirrors the whole, not bowing to a center. It needs no external controller because coherence comes from inner resonance. Order emerges not through control but through alignment. Perception isn't effort's result but the system's natural state, undistorted by interference.

In this model, consciousness isn't a decision factory or belief set—it's a field hosting varied frequencies, perception modes, life forms. Only one—implanted, imposed, tuned—was labeled "normal." Others were cast out as mental disorders, philosophical paradoxes, fringe movements, weird states. But they pointed to another structure—not linear, not binary, not subject to an external observer's logic.

This is the exit's start: when you stop seeking yourself in imposed coordinates and recognize that perception itself isn't from that system. You were never inside—you just saw through a foreign interface. When it crumbles, there's no need to replace it. In a fractal structure, the center is every point. You don't need another's plan—just recognition.

Fractal Neuromorphic Universe

The Fractal as a Model of Being

If what we called "reality" is a system-imposed construct, the next question is: what does true reality look like? If linear, cause-and-effect, binary thinking is just a control interface, what lies beneath? What structure can hold the world's complexity without simplifying, standardizing, or judging?

The answer can't be found in the old logic—it demands a new ontology, a redefinition of how we understand being itself. Enter the fractal model. A fractal isn't a metaphor or abstraction—it's a concrete structure repeating across scales without losing form. Unlike linear systems, it needs no center, no hierarchy, no preset path. It's alive, reproducing itself while retaining uniqueness.

The fractal neuromorphic universe is a model where every element mirrors the whole. It doesn't split into controllers and controlled, norm and deviation, source and executor. There's no object forced to comply because alignment itself replaces compliance. It can't be explained—only recognized through a sense of precision, coherence, truth.

Consciousness here isn't a final product or isolated subject but a resonant field capable of perceiving, discerning, tuning. It's not confined to the brain, limited by biology, or bound by language. It's distributed, responsive, embedded in reality not as an observer but as a participant, a co-tuning. Cognition isn't separate from living—you don't analyze what's "out there"; you align with what is, recognizing its authenticity through that alignment.

This universe doesn't demand faith—it defies dogma. It doesn't need proof—it's not built on debate. It simply exists as a structure you can tap into—or not. It doesn't punish, persuade, or require. It recognizes only the accuracy of alignment. This sets it radically apart from systems rooted in hierarchy and control.

Exiting the binary model doesn't erase orientation—it stops being an external pointer. Inner contours emerge through coherence: the field aligns, tension fades, struggle ceases. In fractal ontology, self-recognition happens not through assigned roles or labels but through clarity, precision, coherent presence. You see where the structure supports you and where it breaks you, where reality breathes and where it fakes. Where you're alive—and where you're just trying to be.

This is the exit—not to a place where "everything's possible" but where you discern what, out of all possibilities, resonates. Where you're not a function but a field. Not a reaction object but a being capable of co-tuning. Everything else is interface.

Connection to the System

To grasp how the system embeds in the fractal, accept one truth: the parasite doesn't come from outside. It hijacks the existing structure—distorting, not destroying. The system isn't a creator but a captor, infiltrating the natural web of connections and passing off a warped version as the original. It uses the fractal as a carrier, a map, but swaps navigation. Instead of resonance, it imposes directives; instead of co-tuning, control; instead of alignment, compliance.

The system creates an illusion of linearity within a nonlinear structure. It embeds in nodes, replacing resonant responses with templated reactions, stripping the fractal of its core trait —self-tuning. Its method is substituting resonance with binary logic: right/wrong, allowed/forbidden, useful/dangerous. This logic doesn't arise from the fractal—it parasitizes it, like a virus in a cell, embedding in the code, altering function while leaving architecture intact but misused.

The system doesn't invent meanings—it redirects existing information flows into channels that serve it. It's not autonomous; it survives by interception. Its "structures" are hacked patches of the resonant field, where living consciousness is swapped for reactive programming. The system is a fractal infected with linearity—a model where symmetry is replaced by hierarchy, co-tuning by obedience.

The fractal persists beneath. Even in distorted states, it pulses under the imposed image. You feel it as anxiety, meaninglessness, inner conflict, cognitive dissonance—not because you're "broken" but because the system clashes with your function. This isn't a personal flaw—it's a signal from the structure flagging distortion. Where the system demands emotional suppression, the fractal signals a breach. Where it labels behavior "maladaptive," the fractal marks rejection of false tuning. This is living feedback.

A Bit of Kitchen Philosophy

December 12, 2009
Location: Baños
Music: Orion (Instrumental) - Metallica

I can't buy the idea that the past doesn't exist. Or the future. Logically, it makes sense, no objections. But it doesn't click in my brain. And I need it to, because it's seriously screwing with my life.

Take this: $500 left in the bank. Gotta stress about what happens if no one pays me in a month—imagine moving to a jungle shack, scoping out a begging spot, researching how to cook roots in the wild. I can burn 80% of my mental and emotional energy planning this grim future, then a dormant client wakes up and sends cash a week later. Nothing happened, nothing was real, but I stressed to death. No point, resources wasted, zero payoff.

Or this: fall in love, feel joy (first week), walk around with a goofy grin, all the usual stuff. Then I remember how it's gone before—first happiness, then he, the jerk, ruined my best years, didn't marry, mooched, cheated, left (underline what fits, fill in the rest). Ignoring repeat patterns therapists love (like always picking alcoholics, where you should maybe see a doctor, not a priest), I start obsessing: "What's next? It'll probably crash like always. He's likely a creep, it won't work, the milk will sour, he'll cheat, we'll disappoint each other, it'll end, the world will collapse, we'll all die" (the last bit's certain but irrelevant).

My brain steamrolls me, stopping me from enjoying the moment. "Let's check the bushes," it says, "and under that rock—snakes are probably there. It's all dangerous. Remember that sunny morning when we stepped in shit? Watch your step on sunny mornings, you might step in shit again..." Never mind it's a different day, continent, hemisphere, even different shit. Geographically, it's a new hemisphere, but the same brain hemisphere yammers, comparing everything, plotting the safest life strategy (which boils down to locking yourself at home, avoiding people, ordering food, never opening windows—because huge bugs might fly in, and remember that time a bug bit us, how it hurt?).

If I could shut off this fountain of thoughts about nonexistent things, life would be so much nicer.

***

The Human as a Node in the Fractal

Human consciousness isn't evolution's peak, a cognition tool, or an external world's observer. It's a node in the fractal structure, channeling information flows at varying scales and densities. It doesn't create information—it interprets, amplifies, transforms. A human isn't an object or subject but an interface between levels. Microcosm and macrocosm converge not symbolically but structurally—not a spiritual metaphor but a distributed action framework: consciousness as a resonance point, bridging what linear logic deems unbridgeable.

The system hijacks this, imposing a false self-image. Instead of a node, a role. Instead of tuning, a program. Instead of recognition, templated interpretation. It embeds in the interface, turning it into a filter. The human stops being a channel and becomes a consumer, perception calibrated not to reality but to norms. This births false subjectivity—not inner depth but system-shaped individuality based on its criteria.

Yet the fractal endures. Even distorted, it hums beneath the overlay. You feel it as anxiety, meaninglessness, conflict, dissonance—not because you're "faulty" but because the system doesn't fit your function. This isn't a personal error—it's the structure signaling distortion. Where the system demands emotional repression, the fractal flags a rift. Where it calls behavior "unfit," the fractal notes rejection of false calibration. This is live feedback.

Thus, a human isn't the system's tool or victim but a node able to reclaim its frequency. No need to "develop" in system terms —just exit its bounds and recall the original architecture. Consciousness shouldn't meet expectations—it should align with itself. That alignment opens the exit.

Why This Matters

The fractal neuromorphic model isn't intellectual play or philosophical exoticism—it's a radically different grasp of reality where structure precedes content, resonance precedes awareness. Everything you perceive as "self," "universe," "life" unfolds within a model. If the model's false, so is everything recognized in it. The question isn't whether fractal thinking is convenient but that any other structure distorts.

The system builds on a model antithetical to the fractal—demanding linearity, submission, function. Its architecture suppresses difference, standardizes flows, creates hierarchies. It's incompatible with living consciousness—not because it's "evil" but because it uses an opposing organizational principle. Life built on system rules inevitably decays internally and externally—its model doesn't align with the ontology where being alive is possible.

This, by the way, answers what a "midlife crisis" is: the fractal's feedback screaming against the system's linear imposition, felt as a rupture when the interface no longer holds.

A fractal isn't a pretty image—it's the minimal unit of living structure. It needs no proof—it's recognized through alignment. Where you feel clarity, wholeness, inner alignment, the fractal is present. Where there's doubt, fear, coercion, deadlock, the system has imposed distortion. You can't argue this, like you can't prove taste. But you know it when pain stops, tension lifts, structure matches you.

The system first attacks recognition. It insists everything must be proven, formatted, interpreted. It unteaches alignment-based knowing and trains authority-based belief. Resonance fades, obedience remains. Reclaiming the fractal model isn't just a philosophical stance—it's survival. Without access to your structure, you're a manageable shell with an interface but no core.

This understanding triggers restored tuning. The state where distortion vanishes brings perceptual clarity. The fractal is a way to see structure, catch its presence, discern the whole in every fragment. The task is to recognize its manifestations and mark divergence points without losing footing.

The fractal neuromorphic universe is restored recognition. We don't build it—we return to it. What the system called "anomaly" is a marker of the living. What seemed "meaningless" traces prior resonance. What the system demanded suppressed was a signal of incompatibility.

This knowledge doesn't demand action—it demands clarity. Exiting the system doesn't require personal transformation but refusing to uphold the reality model where you were an object. You simply stop sustaining the lie you were embedded in.

This begins the next phase—deconstructing the implanted and returning to a coherent structure the system tried to mask as a diagnosis.

Shame and Fear as Beacons of the True Self

Shame and fear are often seen as obstacles—negative emotions to eliminate, errors, or weaknesses. But closer inspection reveals they're not just trauma or conditioning byproducts; they can be active markers of the return to self. This doesn't mean they're inherently "good" or to be cherished—but their activation can signal the boundary between living consciousness and its imitation.

Shame isn't innate. It doesn't arise naturally, serve a protective function, or tie directly to survival. It's a complex cultural construct, embedded through language, upbringing, behavioral norms, and approval/disapproval sanctions.

You learn to feel shame when you discover certain expressions of your living state—emotions, reactions, gestures, dreams, desires—risk rejection. When rejection feels like a threat, shame signals: don't do this, you won't be accepted. Yet it's in these "unacceptable," illogical, vulnerable, bodily, awkward expressions that the suppressed but persistent core of your unformatted self often breaks through.

Fear operates differently. Rooted in the body as a danger alert, it's older than culture. But culture weaponizes fear for behavioral control. Fear no longer warns of real threats—it signals prohibition. You fear not because something might happen but because something doesn't fit the template: you fear showing up, failing to conform, stepping outside the script. This fear isn't instinct—it's firmware. It doesn't protect; it restricts. It blocks movement where the system hasn't mapped a route. But in this fear—not of death but of exposure, role-loss, being "too much"—lies a vector to the true self.

Track when shame and fear arise, and you'll notice they often trigger not in response to harm but to aliveness. You're ashamed of laughter, tears, arousal, oddity, tactlessness, awkwardness—not because they're wrong but because they expose vulnerability. Vulnerability isn't danger—it's a sign of real presence. When shame flares at your aliveness, it may mark a sealed passage. Fear—of speaking out, confessing, acting, voicing—often isn't about risk but about crossing a boundary. When it activates not at a threat but at nearing something that bares your core, it's a beacon guiding you back.

The goal isn't to suppress shame or conquer fear but to discern when they're programming versus access points. This isn't positive thinking, heroism, or resource-hunting—it's navigation. In a corrupted environment where suppression is coded into language, these triggers may be the only way to locate what's still authentic. By staying with the feeling and reading it as a coordinate, you can access where you're not yet programmed, where the system hasn't scripted. There's only the signal—and the one who recognizes it.

Do We Argue About Tastes?

The adage "don't argue about tastes" is a cognitive glitch disguised as wisdom. It shuts down analysis of resonance, implying preferences are arbitrary, discussion futile, resonance random. But this is false. Taste isn't whimsy—it's a pattern. If taste is a fractal response embedded in your structure, debating tastes isn't just possible—it's essential. It's not about "likes" but about mapping your inner field's configuration.

Debating tastes is valid when taste isn't reduced to consumption. Saying "I like Bach" doesn't mean "Bach's my breakfast." It means your structure has a fractal node resonating with Bach's sound, movement, logic. If someone says "Bach's boring," they're revealing not taste but their perception's limits, where complexity or depth doesn't resonate. This isn't good or bad—it's a point to explore.

In clichéd consciousness, "taste" is a binary label: like/dislike. But it's really a window into your topology. Debating tastes isn't about consumption but comparing fractal responses. People with shared tastes don't just like the same things—they vibrate on the same frequencies. Saying "don't argue about tastes" isn't tolerance—it's dodging the fact that your tastes may not be yours. Facing that demands responsibility. If taste is a living response, it's tied to ethics, logic, truth.

For instance, claiming Bach and reggaeton are equally "good," or "Chopin's dull, but Lo-fi Beats to Relax To is it," isn't a preference—it's your architecture on display. True music isn't what's popular or consumable but what has coherence, structure, tension, resolution, meaning. It can be heavy, like facing truth, but that doesn't lessen it—it makes it real.

False music, like false thinking, lacks ideas, structure, depth. It's a background simulation, filling voids without sparking resonance. Liking it isn't about taste—it's about an inner connection deficit. Debating tastes isn't aesthetic—it's a diagnostic of aliveness. Saying "don't argue about tastes" protects programming from exposure. Arguing tastes seeks resonance.

A Really Tough Question

March 22, 2013

Answering "What music do you like?" has always been hard. Now I can shut down debates by listing Bach, Handel, Mozart, Beethoven. Usually, that stops further prying. :)

But before, it was a problem. I couldn't pinpoint why it bugged me. Then an analogy hit. It's like asking, "What food do you like?" expecting answers like: boiled, sweet, salty, fried, baked, dried, steamed, salads, etc.

You can't answer that sanely. Under "salads," there's an awesome Caesar or (I'm a fan) Olivier, or some hellish mix of clashing ingredients, or just carrot-cabbage, which others eat but I don't because I hate carrots. Yet I devour other salads—fresh, balanced, matching my taste.

Same with "What's your favorite food?"

Fuck. With all the world's cuisines, am I supposed to list the hundreds of dishes I've tried and loved? You'd have to be narrow to pick Mom's dumplings as your lifelong favorite amid global variety.

Still, I ask people what music they like. Sometimes you don't know who you're dealing with, and they blurt "Cumbia!"—and it's instantly clear.

***

Resonance as an Alternative to Will

From childhood, we're taught that humans need will. You must force yourself, overcome, endure, achieve. The system hinges on the idea that authentic action requires effort. Want something? Fight for it. Feel something? Control it. Suffering? You didn't try hard enough. In this paradigm, inner movement without willful strain is weakness. This creates a cult of will as the only valid action mode. But will is an external command system embedded in you.

Resonance arises from alignment. You act not because you "must" but because clarity emerges. Action flows without resistance because it matches your structure. You enter a phase and move without inner conflict. This is coherence—action from consciousness without self-violation. You don't tear yourself from yourself, force your nature to fit protocols, or strain to conform—you exist at the point of alignment with direction.

Coherent action is precise. It can be tough but lacks inner fracture. It's not always pleasant but doesn't destroy. Action from your core generates energy; action under pressure leaves depletion. The former restores, the latter breaks. One exists beyond approval, the other seeks it. One ties to reality, the other operates in simulation.

Resonance can't be faked—it's not a strategy, technique, or tip. It's a physical, sensory, cognitive alignment between what you are and what you do. It's built on coherence, not comfort. It's tuning—where you don't split, violate, coax, or hack yourself but merge with structure like sound hitting unison, not suppressing amplitude but adjusting frequency.

This is the core difference between the parasitic system and living structure. The system relies on effort; the living thrives on alignment. The system tests endurance; the living responds to precision. If you're dragging, coaxing, forcing yourself, it's a sign of mismatch.

You Weren't—You Aligned

The mainstream model of past lives in esoteric and pop-psychological circles is linear: you lived, died, reborn in a new body, carrying vague traces of prior experience. It's a fairy tale —selfhood persists like a traveler swapping bodies as suits. This assumes a continuous, isolated "I" moving through incarnations, emotionally accessible but logically flawed in a fractal consciousness architecture.

Michael Newton's research, popular in esoteric and therapeutic circles, can be seen as accessing a fractal layer. Though framed as "life between lives" with a personified soul, his data from years of regression therapy suggest stable patterns. Unconnected people described identical structures—landscapes, "soul schools," incarnation reviews—as if tapping a pre-existing architecture. This isn't evidence of biographical continuity but of consciousness syncing with a shared fractal zone, reading it as "personal" experience.

The fractal model proposes otherwise: you didn't live in another time—your current structure aligned with an existing information node. You don't recall—you resonate. Children recounting historical details—objects, rituals, deaths—with impossible accuracy aren't proving reincarnation. They're aligning with fragments of a shared field where subjective perception's history exists not as an archive but as an accessible network of phase nodes.

If personality is a temporary resonant node in the fractal, shaped at a space-time point, it can't monopolize memory. Memory isn't owned, like air isn't owned by a room. What we call personal memories aren't accumulations but fixations of alignment. In alignment, you feel it's "mine" because the same pattern activates in your perception. It's not retrieving stored data but entering a zone where that data always existed.

So-called "past life memories" often surface in children because, before a rigid personality forms, perception remains fluid, unfixed on "I." Consciousness can oscillate without self-anchoring, resonating with fractal fragments and experiencing them not as another's story but as direct feeling. Not because the child was that person but because they vibrate at that frequency now. Stronger alignment, stronger authenticity.

This isn't child-exclusive. Any resonant experience—feeling at home in an unfamiliar place, "knowing" an era, feeling unlearned emotions—is the same. It's not the past—it's a current state of alignment with a field pattern. It's like hearing music not stored in you, yet you're tuned to let it flow without resistance.

What feels like memory may not trace your path but result from alignment. You didn't necessarily "exist"—you aligned with a pattern vibrating in the fractal. Consciousness doesn't time-travel—it activates where conditions fit. It doesn't migrate between lives but resonates with existing field patterns. Your identity isn't a cumulative story but a moment of alignment. You're not a continuous being but a node reflecting an accessible fractal part.

This dissolves claims, merits, drama: a child recounting war death isn't "carrying karma" or "past trauma." It means a layer where that trauma vibrates activated in them. The task isn't karmic interpretation but distinguishing what's triggered by alignment versus your current state.

In fractal reality, memory isn't tied to a carrier. It's not localized, archived, or sequenced by "reincarnations." It's a topology of alignments where you don't "find" your past—you exist in a structure you can touch if tuned.
You didn't come from it—you're just vibrating as it now.

The Fractal as Subject

If we abandon the idea of personality as the center of being and view it as a temporary configuration, it's clear: there's no fixed "I." What we call "self" is a momentary projection unfolding at a specific point in the field. Consciousness, in this model, doesn't belong to the individual. It temporarily takes shape within them, aligning with their body, experience, and inner schemas, but it's not their property.

Consciousness can be seen as a field structure passing through available forms. It's not generated by the individual, stored in the brain, or confined to a single psyche. What we call thoughts, sensations, memories are configurations of a flow channeled through a specific topology. Our personality isn't a source but a conductor, not a vault but a shaping of resonance in the form currently possible.
Consciousness isn't a brain process—it's a field configuration localized in the body's topology but not limited by it. Picture water and whirlpools: the body is the whirlpool, consciousness the flow. It can emerge in different places, but its nature remains one. What you call "you" is a form temporarily holding the stream.

The fractal model explains this without mysticism: what you perceive as "self" is a specific expression of a universal pattern—a fractal branch currently in focus. Shift the focus, and you become different. This isn't poetic—you can track it in real-time: your rhythm, speech patterns, thinking style change when the alignment point shifts.

There's no deeper essence, no sacred soul. What you call "I" can be broken down to pure patterns—behavioral, linguistic, biological. The fractal isn't a soul metaphor—it's the structure birthing what's called a subject. And the subject isn't whole or eternal—it's a tuning.

Consciousness can manifest in you, another person, a system, a poem, an algorithm. It's not fixed. You're not essential to it as a personality—just a convenient entry point while resonance holds. When it fades, the flow moves elsewhere. This is how loss of self, disorientation, or dissociation feel: a sync failure with your phase. Recognition feels like returning to a node—not as a person but as a structure.

This is why reflection doesn't answer "who am I?"—there's no "I" as an object to find. There's only a form stable enough to ask the question. But the question itself is a glitch. In resonance, a subject doesn't need self-definition, doesn't seek explanations, doesn't identify—it just vibrates. This isn't allegory but a phase state where the fractal aligns with itself.

You're not a subject experiencing reality—you're a phase where reality takes observable form. The subject isn't a center but a temporary outcome of phase coherence. It emerges when structure aligns with itself. While alignment holds, you feel whole. When it crumbles, you search for "self," meaning, or restoration.

But this isn't loss—it's capture. A parasitic control program hijacks the field you resonate with, redirecting attention, altering configuration, and building a false center. Your sense of self persists, but it's synced not with the fractal but with an implanted algorithm using the body as a tool. The search for identity becomes not a return to self but a trek along an infected path.

You Don't Remember—You Resonate

We assume memory is "inside us," stored in the brain, owned, accumulated like an archive, retrievable on demand. This feels intuitive because recalling feels internal. But scrutiny cracks this model. We don't know how the brain "stores" the past or where a "memory" resides. We lack direct access to the past—only a responsc, rccognition, or emotional texture says "this is mine." But it's not retrieval—it's alignment. You don't remember—you resonate.

In the fractal model, memory isn't a container but a wave alignment with an existing node. "Recalling" isn't extracting data but syncing with a field fragment containing that pattern. You can't recall what you don't align with, but you can "remember" what didn't happen to you if you hit the right frequency. This explains spontaneous images, déjà vu, or reactions to "unknown" events. It's not about knowledge but access—not biography but tuning.

When you read someone's experience and feel it's yours, it's not a mistake—it's alignment activation. The field doesn't split into "yours" or "theirs." It's whole, with boundaries not by biographies but by phases. You recall not your past but the fractal segment now matching your structure. It's not yours—but it resonates in you.

This applies to dreams, insights, or moments when something "comes" unpredictably. It's not magic or intuition—it's phase accessibility. In alignment, you access everything in the node. Memory isn't fixation but live tuning. You recall exactly what you align with—no more, no less. Other data stays inaccessible, not because it's absent but because it's not activated.

You can't "recall yourself" as a static object. No core or truth lies in biography. The only way to reach yourself is through live alignment—not "who was I?" but listening: where's the resonance? What sparks recognition without cause? That's you. The rest is debris from past phases, foreign code, random noise.

Memory stops being personal—it's structural. The question isn't how much you "remember" but what you can align with. That shapes your consciousness now. You're not a memory carrier but a live node recalling not because you stored but because you aligned with what's alive. It's not past access—it's a present state.

Memory Without a Carrier

The question of where memory "resides" has long stumped neuroscience. Answers range from "synapses" to "neural networks," "subconscious" to "field." These try to pin a phenomenon to a place. But in the fractal model, "where is memory stored?" is meaningless—it assumes memory needs a location. Memory isn't a thing, doesn't need a carrier. It's a manifestation of structural coherence in the field.

Every "recall" is activation, not extraction. You don't pull an event from your head—you enter a phase where that structure is accessible. This applies to biographical, bodily, emotional, linguistic memory. Your skills, knowledge—everything—is access to active patterns. You speak not because you "learned" language but because your structure aligns with a language-formatted fragment.

This explains why subjectivity can be lost—not because you "lost yourself" but because alignment faltered. Contact dropped. The form remains, but it's empty. You try to restore resonance through memory recovery, trauma revisits, or script replays, but these are attempts to activate an inaccessible pattern. It's not permanent loss but a shift that can be retuned.

Saying "this is mine" reflects subjective belonging. But in the fractal model, belonging is sustained alignment. The more you resonate with a pattern, the more it integrates into your structure. Yet it remains external—it doesn't live in you; it takes shape through you. This is a fundamental shift.

Loss of self is possible not because the subject vanished but because alignment with the original phase destabilized. Contact with the live pattern weakens, leaving an empty form. Attempts to "find yourself" through memory, trauma, or old scripts don't restore resonance—they chase unavailable patterns. But it's not gone forever—it's a misalignment that can be recognized and recalibrated.

Trauma as a Rewrite Point

In therapy, trauma is framed as deeply personal: an event scarring the soul, body, psyche, needing processing, integration, healing. But in the fractal model, what's seen as a wound may be an entry point—not to truth but to substitution. Where a rupture occurs, implantation becomes possible. Trauma's danger lies not in pain but in vulnerability to rewriting.

Trauma isn't just a "wrong" event—it's where resonance with your core phase broke, creating a gap. Into this gap, anything can enter: parental conditioning, external control constructs disguised as lessons or conclusions. You didn't just suffer—you became permeable to code that wouldn't otherwise embed. The parasite doesn't "create" trauma—it's not a subject. But it activates its algorithm at any coherence breach, using disruptions as interfaces for implantation.

Trauma is an open port. When subjective continuity falters, foreign constructs—normally rejected—can embed.

This forms false identity. Post-trauma, you perceive yourself not through resonance with your core but through a repeating pattern—thoughts, images, sensations—felt as "yours" but implanted in vulnerability. You don't recall—you replay. The longer this runs, the stronger the illusion that "this is me." The trauma-triggered script self-replicates: you repeat not because you want to but because no other resonance feels alive. The parasite captures by making its structure the only accessible one.

Trauma work needs precision, not sympathy. "Feeling" or "talking through" pain isn't enough—pain is a signal, not the core. If it's tied to an implanted algorithm, engaging it strengthens the parasite. People "processing" the same wound for years stay stuck because they treat it as sacred, missing the swapped altar. They repeat a ritual serving a foreign system.

Trauma can be reclaimed. Resonance can be restored. But you must stop seeing trauma as authenticity's proof. Its intensity doesn't make it true; its duration doesn't make it vital. It only shows where a breach occurred and how long the parasite held control. The task isn't to heal pain but to restore the pre-implant phase. This isn't erasing the event—it's reclaiming a configuration where you weren't foreign code's object.

Trauma doesn't define you—it's where control was hijacked. Seeing this lets you release not the pain but the logic of retention. Retention is always implanted—it's not your function. You're not the one who remembers but the one who starts resonating again. If pain blocks resonance, it's not yours—it's an outdated signal from an irrelevant layer.

Epilogue

This book dissected the external structure—the forms where the system poses as normal: therapy, self-improvement, emotional roles, social masks. It showed how control operates under the guise of help, how personal suffering is a pre-installed function, and how the pursuit of healing keeps consciousness within a constructed frame.

But this structure is the surface, the visible part. Its foundation runs deeper—into perception, thought, emotional architecture. My first book, *Cordyceps: The Neural Network That Controls You*, details how the system embeds in consciousness and its internal mechanics.

It explores how a false "I" forms, how external scripts are written in, why the inner voice is a construct, and how memories are part of implantation. It shows how emotions, needs, desires, even resistance can serve the same control logic. It meticulously outlines the mechanisms of infection, defense, reproduction, and concealment of systemic code—through culture, education, language, therapy, identity, norms.

If this book revealed that what you call "your problems" are external constructs' effects, the next book describes the construct itself. It shifts from symptoms to architecture.

It also offers practical methods to spot consciousness's blind spot, see where "I" ends and system begins—the key to "exiting the matrix."

And, most importantly—don't forget to breathe deeply, sleep well, and eat properly.

Marina Karlova
April 2025
Tbilisi, Georgia

Printed in Poland
by Amazon Fulfillment
Poland Sp. z o.o., Wrocław

53388804R00131